# See Jane Fly

"As a teenager, Nicole Kluemper became the most famous case of recovered memory, thanks to a recording of her recovering a memory of sexual abuse. Or did she? Had she been abused by her mother years before? As a young woman, Kluemper was subjected to unethical, traumatic, and prolonged abuses of power by a famous memory researcher who denies that recovered memories exist. She was robbed of her confidentiality and privacy, nearly destroyed by legal battles, and ultimately robbed of the possibility of assessing the reality of her own memories. But finally, with this courageous and at times searingly honest book, she has found her voice and claimed her story."

**—Jim Hopper**, PhD

"This book speaks volumes to an individual's abilities to persist in the face of a formidable adversary, and to transform trauma into power. Anyone who works with survivors should read this book, for two reasons. First, to witness Dr. Kluemper's courage. Second, to familiarize yourself with the behaviors of the pseudonymous psychologist who pursued Dr. Kluemper as if she were in some way to blame for what happened to her. I only wish that it were safe for that person to be named."

**—Laura S. Brown**, PhD, ABPP

"*See Jane Fly* is a gripping account of Nicole Kluemper's extraordinary experiences as an unwitting subject of privacy invasion and intrusion at the hands of certain professors and journalists. Kluemper's personal experiences were fought over by strangers who used her case to argue for or against the possibility of relatively accurate recovered memories. Kluemper handled this injustice and intrusion with remarkable courage and strength, repeatedly speaking truth to power while becoming first a Navy pilot and then a licensed clinical psychologist. In this insightful and moving memoir, Kluemper conveys with remarkable honesty both the pain of injustice and the power of fiercely won triumphs."

—**Jennifer Joy Freyd**, PhD, Founder and President,
   Center for Institutional Courage; Professor Emerit,
   Psychology, University of Oregon; Adjunct Professor,
   Psychiatry and Behavioral Sciences, Stanford University;
   Editor, *Journal of Trauma & Dissociation*

"You may think it would be painful to read a book that, at first glance, seems full of grief. But keep in mind that the relief that comes from sharing grief is compelling. Nicole finds joy in a drop of honeysuckle nectar on her tongue, which helps her bear the venom from her foster mother's nagging tongue. Nicole takes 'courage' out of 'discourage.' This book is a tribute to never giving up."

—**Ellen Nichols**, Author of
   *Remember Whose Little Girl You Are*

a memoir

NICOLE S. KLUEMPER, PHD

VIRGINIA BEACH
CAPE CHARLES

See Jane Fly

by Nicole S. Kluemper, PhD

ISBN 978-1-64663-893-2

Published by

 köehlerbooks™

3705 Shore Drive
Virginia Beach, VA 23455
800-435-4811
www.koehlerbooks.com

*To my father and my husband*

*Although your paths never crossed,*
*I am convinced you are kindred souls.*
*Thank you for all you have done for me*
*and for all your love has allowed me to do.*

# Author's Note

Some of the names in this book have been changed in order to protect the privacy of those involved. Accusations of wrongdoing or unprofessional behavior recounted in these pages have been alleged in multiple court proceedings, before ethical review panels, or expressed in professional journals.

The following is a list of fictitious names: Dr. Malvonia East, Dr. Evillene Thropp, Igor Petty, Dr. Green, Helga, Deirdre, Agnes, Amy, Karen, George, Stacy, Pam, Stan, Kurt, Justine, Gabe, Steve, Tammy, Katherine, Captain Henry, Captain Roberts, MMC Davidson, Narcissa, Liam, Dick, Rebecca, Colleen, Susie, Kate, Professor Jones, Valerie, Anna, Andi, Dr. Cobb, CDR Williams, CDR Lewis, and CDR Morris.

# Table of Contents

# Prologue

Either I was molested in a bathtub by my biological mother as a four-year-old child, or I wasn't. Sitting here today, I honestly have no idea which version of events is true. A court-appointed, impartial, forensic evaluator, Dr. David Corwin, made video recordings of me saying I was hurt by my biological mother in no uncertain terms. Dr. Corwin believed me and made his recommendation to a judge based on the data he collected. The judge gave full custody to my father, William Taus, at a time when this was uncommon. I grew up with my dad, feeling loved and doted on. Who cares that I will never know the truth about this one detail of my life?

Well, I do.

When I was approximately ten years old, my dad and I agreed to allow my information to be used for Dr. Corwin's training/lectures. Then, as a seventeen-year-old, I had a memory recall of the sexual abuse, which was also video recorded by Dr. Corwin. I was told this type of recording was a first, and asked if I would agree to allow my case to be used for the purpose of informing other mental health professionals. I agreed to participate in the case report anonymously. No one was ever supposed to know who I was. I was given the name "Jane Doe" in an attempt to hide my true identity. Small details regarding my life were changed. I'll say it again—no one was ever supposed to know who I was.

Dr. Corwin was confident he could maintain my privacy, and I was not given any indication there was reason to suspect otherwise.

Researchers often ask people to share very private parts of their lives in the name of science, and the notion that they would retain privacy is sometimes the only reason they would participate. Removing this promise of confidentiality would mean many potential participants in case reports or other research would decline consent to allowing their information to be used for further scientific study.

Dr. Malvonia East (not her real name), a memory researcher, chose to hire a private investigator and uncover my identity when I was nineteen years old. Her actions created additional trauma in my life. I felt like a football in a game I didn't want to be playing. Parts of my life were being used to make or break psychological theories. Had my identity remained secret, the use of my information as part of the debate would not have been problematic for me. As an expert witness in *other* cases, Dr. East was bombarded with questions about *my* case report on the witness stand, or so I've been told. The facts of my case tended to disprove one of her hypotheses, which is that memory cannot reliably be recovered in its true form once forgotten. Dr. East made me an identifiable public figure, using one of the most traumatic events in my life, when all I wanted was to remain unknown. She took control of my life story, and to this day, she is unapologetic about it. The trauma attributed to Dr. East's actions in court records far exceeds that of the possible abuse attributed to in my judicial cases to my biological mother.

So much commentary and opinion have been expressed by both experts and the media on this part of my life—I will never know for sure what really happened to me. I have participated in interviews and conference presentations with one singular goal in mind—to stop any mental health professional from ever doing this to anyone else.

In attempting to tell my story, I'm trying to regain power over my narrative. I'd like to set the stage by differentiating between the terms *repressed* and *recovered* memory. There are essentially two sides in the debate regarding memory. Those who use the term *recovered memory* are typically of the opinion that memory can be forgotten and recalled reliably over time. Those who believe that forgotten or repressed memories cannot later be remembered reliably often use the term *repressed memory* instead.

# CHAPTER ONE

# The Accident

"This is Dr. Green, calling from VacaValley Hospital. I'm afraid your dad has been in an accident, and you should get here as soon as possible."

I stood in the spare bedroom while the voice on the answering machine kept talking, I didn't hear the rest. My mind was racing with a million questions all at once. Did they know my dad had suffered a minor stroke a few months ago while he was painting the living room? How on earth could they know? If they did know, would it make a difference? What was the extent of his injuries?

Who should I call to get a ride to the hospital? Should I try to contact the hospital first? Who else do I need to talk to?

As I stood there, I looked down at my hand. I realized, while I was holding the telephone receiver, my hand shook. I took a breath and closed my eyes tight.

The unwanted message shattered what had been an otherwise normal day in the life of a twelve-year-old. My friend Amy and I had walked to her boyfriend George's house from school. My dad had agreed to pick Amy and me up at dinnertime. When he didn't show up, we called and waited, and when it got late, Stacy's mom saw us waiting and offered to drive us to my house.

I went immediately to the spare bedroom, where we kept the answering machine, hoping for a message from my dad explaining his absence. I saw the blinking light on the answering machine and pushed the button, expecting to hear my dad's voice. Instead,

I heard the message from Dr. Green; my dad had a stroke, and he was in the hospital in a coma.

I let out a small sob, then felt the panic rise from deep within me. Amy put a hand on my shoulder to steady me. My eyes met hers, and I handed her the phone, hoping she had someone to call who could give us a ride to see my dad. All I could think about now was getting to my dad, and I was terrified I might not have a chance to say goodbye.

My father was fifty-two when I was born, while my mother was twenty years his junior. My father had a daughter and son from a previous marriage. He divorced their mother once they were adults. According to all involved, they disowned him when he decided to leave New York and move to California. My mother had one son from her previous marriage, and she was born and raised in Northern California.

I understood from a young age that my dad was older than most dads. When I would go places with my father, people used to mistake him for my grandfather. At first, I didn't understand the implication. Once I understood, I started to hate it when people made this mistake. It made me uncomfortable to see my father embarrassed, and it embarrassed me too. It made me want to hide behind him and wait for the encounter to be over so I could slink away. My dad always appeared to take it in stride. He would smile wide and make a joke or laugh it off, then move the conversation along to a safer topic.

I first became fearful he was going to die when I was about seven years old. One of the neighborhood moms asked me about it.

"Do you ever worry your dad is going to die?"

I was rarely at a loss for words as a child. This question left me speechless.

"Not to be mean," this woman continued, "he's really old for a dad."

I considered the age of each of the dads in the neighborhood in turn. The woman was right. I had never carried this thought forward to the obvious conclusion before. This meant he was going to die sooner than the other dads.

"Well, I just think you should be prepared for it," the woman concluded, and then went about washing her car.

I was horror-struck. I walked home in a daze, went to my bedroom, closed the door, and wept. To my mind, my dad had just been given a death sentence. My world would never be the same again.

From then on, I carried with me the fear of losing my dad. I would lie in bed at night, role-playing possible scenarios in which I found out my dad had died. This made me feel horrible.

Later in life, I understood this was my way of preparing myself for a time when my father would no longer be present. I couldn't stop thinking about my dad's advanced age. These were the thoughts I had as Amy's grandfather drove us to the hospital.

My dad had been driving his brown 1983 Chevy Cavalier hatchback at the time of his accident. A stroke caused him to lose consciousness and run into a car stopped at a stoplight. He hit the windshield, shattering it. It left a large hematoma on his forehead. I had never seen anything like it before; it was four inches across and filled with fluid, swaying like a waterbed when I touched it. The emergency-room doctor quickly explained that this seemed to be his only major injury, and it could have been so much worse.

After a while, the doctor's speech mixed together, making sounds that no longer resembled words. I did hear the doctor tell me if my dad woke up, he would "either live four days or four years." I was terrified. I was twelve years old and in seventh grade. He was speaking to me as though I was a responsible adult. I remember thinking to myself, *Who says that to a child whose father is lying in a hospital bed?*

The thought remained unspoken because I just didn't have the emotional energy to deal with a doctor with such terrible bedside manner. I turned to my dad and looked at him; I was helpless. I felt tears stream down my face. I wished I could take back every harsh word and every rude comment I had ever spoken to him. I wanted to ball up my fists and bang on his chest, scream at him until he woke up. I wanted to curl up next to him, pull his arm over me, let his fate be my fate. I wanted to be anyone other than the twelve-year-old standing here alone, wondering whether my only parent was going to live or die.

Two days later, my dad did wake up. Not long after, he developed an infection in his bloodstream, which caused a high fever and another coma. The attending doctor called and told me my father was going to die, and to come to the hospital to say my goodbyes.

My friend's parents were doing what they could to help. My friend George's mother, Karen, gave me a ride to the hospital. I stood over my father's bed, and I was shocked to see his tongue clipped to his lower lip. I asked a nurse why. She gently explained, "Honey, this is to keep him from swallowing it in case he has another seizure." She continued, "He's also on an ice blanket, to help control the fever." All I saw was a white sheet draped over his small frame, the tubes, and wires coming from his hand and chest.

I told the nurse I didn't know what to do or how to say goodbye. She looked at me and simply said, "Just talk to him, sweetheart."

So, I talked. I said whatever came to my mind. I told him I loved him, and I wasn't ready for him to go. I told him how sorry I was for the fights and the unfinished chores, and I promised him I'd fulfill his dream; I'd grow up to be *more than he was.*

My dad always said, "Be more than I was." It was hard for me to understand as a young child because I thought there was no job cooler than playing with sparkly jewels all day. My dad had to explain to me that he was a diamond setter by trade, and he never went to college. He didn't really have specific ideas about a profession for me. He just wanted *more* for me—for me to be more than he was and for me to achieve more than he could.

My dad and I were close, though, like most kids, I argued with him about chores. My dad didn't have much extra money when I was growing up. He always found a way to send me to Girl Scout horse camp during the summer. I looked forward to going to horse camp each summer, as this was my only opportunity to ride. We learned to muck the stalls, saddle the horses, and ride trails. I enjoyed the closeness and comradery with the other campers. The second summer, I got very sick. I couldn't keep anything down. It was odd because no one else in the entire camp was sick. The camp counselors let me call my dad each evening. After hearing my dad's voice, suddenly, my stomach would calm. Knowing he was no more than a phone call away made me feel less anxious. After three days of a week-long camp, I was still not able to keep anything in my stomach. My camp counselors decided that my dad needed to come pick me up. As soon as he got there, I was fine. I had missed him so much, it made me sick.

Anytime we were apart, I sang a song about the two of us looking up at the same moon to make myself feel better. My dad was my safe place, my best friend, and my inspiration.

On the drive home from the hospital, after saying goodbye to my dad, a popular song came on the radio in which the singer lamented his ability to "say goodbye to yesterday." I prayed a simple prayer, telling God how I wasn't ready for my dad to leave yet, and I just knew my dad was going to survive the night.

I went to George's house and sat by the phone.

A few hours later, I got a call from a nurse at the hospital. When she had gone to suction out my dad's lungs to make him comfortable, my dad opened his eyes and asked for a sponge bath. That sounded just like my dad to me. I felt as though God had answered my prayer, and I was thankful we would have more time together.

# CHAPTER TWO

# The Accusation

When I was five years old, my biological mother, Deirdre, and my father were in the middle of an ugly divorce. The court had already ordered shared custody, and I spent half of my time at each house. After a visit to Deidre's house, I told my dad and the woman who would become my stepmother, Agnes, about something that happened in the bathtub. I said Deirdre had put her fingers in my vagina while bathing me and asked me if it felt good. Not surprisingly, Deirdre denied this, and the back and forth between my dad and Deirdre through the courts ensued.

Forensic exams of my body were ordered by the court.

Following one visit to Deirdre's house, I returned to my dad's home with large blisters on the bottom of both feet and the palm of my left hand. My dad and Agnes took photos of my feet and hand with the blisters, the origin of which were never determined.

My dad fought hard to get custody of me. There were two court cases being conducted sequentially. One in the superior court, and the other in family court. The family court judge ordered an unbiased third-party supervised visit with Deirdre, while the superior court judge's order allowed Deirdre's mother to supervise the visitation. My dad followed the order of the family court. The superior court judge summoned him, found him in contempt, and ordered him to be held in jail. I remember running back and forth with Agnes, getting copies of the family court order, communicating with my dad's lawyer, and taking my dad a fresh suit and shave kit the following morning. My father appeared once again, this time with his lawyer, before the superior court judge, who promptly released him. The judges of the superior and family courts later convened and decided to never let such a thing happen again. Even at the time, I knew my dad didn't have to fight as hard as he did for custody of me.

The court appointed a psychiatrist named David Corwin to conduct a forensic evaluation. Based on the results of his investigation, Dr. Corwin recommended my father get full custody and my mother have supervised visitation. I was raised by my dad, and he was my best friend. Over time, Deirdre faded from my life.

Agnes and my dad were business partners, and she became his third and last wife. They worked a jewelry repair shop out of our home in one of the spare bedrooms. Agnes was an animated and charismatic woman. I idolized her. I would dress up like her and try to act like her. At age six, dressed in a pretty rose-pink gown, I served as a flower girl in their wedding. This would turn out to be a short-lived attachment.

By the time I turned eight years old, my dad and Agnes had divorced. They continued to work the jewelry business together. A few months later, my dad went into the hospital for prostate surgery. The doctors found that he needed double bypass open-heart surgery during the pre-op testing. Agnes called the hospital and told the doctors that my father didn't have health insurance and encouraged them not to do the surgery. While I'm not certain this tactic could have worked, the idea of a former spouse attempting to stop lifesaving surgery is appalling.

While my dad was in the hospital having surgery, I stayed at a neighbor's house. Agnes came to the neighbor's house and rang the bell.

"Hello," the neighbor greeted Agnes at the door.

"Hi," Agnes said. "Please have Nicole gather her things. Her dad wants her to come with me."

"Oh?" the neighbor said. "Is everything alright?"

"Yes," said Agnes. "She just needs to get her things together and come with me now."

I still had a great deal of affection for Agnes, so I did as she said with no questions asked. Agnes drove me to a neighboring city and dropped me off at Child Haven. This was short-term group home typically for children removed from their parents' care due to neglect or other abuse.

I stood and watched as a cot was set up in the middle of a common area for me to sleep on. It was already dark, and the other children in the facility were asleep. I would only spend one night there. I still recall this as one of the most terrifying nights of my life. I had no idea what was going on.

The next day, Agnes brought in a moving truck and removed every last item from our home, leaving only vacant rooms.

My dad must have called to say good night to me at the neighbor's house where he left me, and when he found out I wasn't there, he made sure I was moved from Child Haven the following day. I ended up at the home of my longtime babysitter, Pam, and I knew I would be safe there until my dad got home.

My dad had to come home to an empty house less than a week after having open-heart surgery. The neighbors and I all thought he was going to have a heart attack right then and there.

We stood outside our white house, in the center of our cul-de-sac, waiting for some signal to tell us the time was right to go inside. Knowing what to expect, my dad gave us the go-ahead.

I straggled behind the line of adults marching dutifully across the front lawn and toward the door. Someone had unlocked the house, so the adults fell in single file now, each passing through the doorway with a worried, if not horrified, expression on their face. I followed behind, and I was still standing in the entryway when the adults reached the empty kitchen. The sight of it gave me a start. Not a cup nor a spoon remained. The refrigerator was empty.

The bare kitchen gave way to the vacant living room, the biggest room of the house. The indentations in the carpet where the couch feet had stood were the only indication any furniture had ever been there at all.

One by one, the four of them walked through the house, always with me tagging along. The workshop in which my dad and Agnes had worked together was empty. The entire inventory was gone.

There was not a bed, a dresser, or so much as a piece of clothing left behind. I stepped into my bedroom, and everything was gone, including my favorite yellow bedtime bunny. My dad borrowed two blow-up mattresses and some blankets from the neighbors for the night.

My dad slowly bought used furniture from Goodwill and secondhand stores. He went to court, and a year later, Agnes was required to return half of what she had taken.

Over the years, my dad and I recovered from Agnes's departure emotionally too. I remember summertime trips to the community swimming pool with my dad, during which I would beg him for money to buy Red Vines and try to abide by the "no running" rule as I made my way to the snack bar to retrieve my treasure. For my eleventh birthday, he drove me to Disneyland for the park's thirty-fifth anniversary. His car broke down in the middle of nowhere, and we had to call his best friend, Stan, to rescue us. My dad got us a fish tank, and we struggled to keep the thing clean and the poor fish alive. These are some of the happiest memories of my life.

I remember sitting on my dad's bed in our old house, watching *Top Gun* together as we so often did. My dad told me he wanted to be a pilot. He was supposed to join the Army, but he switched to the Navy at the last minute because the recruiter told him there was a *chance* he could fly, even though he wore glasses. My dad became an aircraft mechanic in the Navy. He always regretted his choice. Later, he found out Army pilots were allowed to fly with glasses, while Navy pilots still needed twenty-twenty vision.

One evening, very much enjoying the adrenaline high from the final *Top Gun* aerial dogfighting scene, I told my dad I would fulfill his dream of flying for him. While I couldn't say for sure I truly meant those words as I spoke them, later, the dream would become very, very real.

# Jumping Around

When my father had his stroke while driving, Deirdre was no longer in my life, nor was anyone from her side of the family. My father had become estranged from his family members when he chose to move to California from New York. There was no family for me to live with. While my dad was in a convalescent hospital, I finished eighth grade and half of ninth grade. I moved six times between the homes of several friends and acquaintances, then into group homes. Moving between so many different houses was extremely difficult for me.

George, my best friend Amy's boyfriend, lived with his mom, Karen, his stepfather, and four siblings in a four-bedroom house. On the way back from the hospital the first night, Karen offered to let me stay with her family. I was thankful. As the days and weeks passed, it became clear this had become an unexpected long-term arrangement.

I slept on a pullout bed in the bedroom of their six-year-old daughter, Rebecca. Karen didn't miss an opportunity to tell me how "unfair" it was that Rebecca had to share her room with me. I was not allowed to have anything of mine out on display in the room. I was instructed to keep my belongings put away, because it was Rebecca's room, not mine.

From my point of view, I had gone from being the only child of a doting father to a second thought by anyone who would deign to allow me to stay with them. I was also going through the typical first crush, first kiss, and first boyfriend angst in the midst of all of the moving. I remember this time as one of the most confusing periods in my life.

Karen helped clean out my father's house, preparing it to be sold. While she packed and sorted, I wasn't allowed to be there. This was the final piece of the life I had had with my father. Even at twelve years old, I knew my life would never be the same.

I remember being at my father's house just before it was sold, and the boy I was dating, Kurt, met me there. He rode his bike all the way across town and snuck into the backyard. Amidst the twenty-two fruit trees my dad had planted in the backyard were tall weeds Kurt had to forge a path through. He met me at the sliding glass door in my dad's old bedroom. He could see I was shaken and asked me if I was alright. I lied and told him I was, and we exchanged a few other words. We heard someone coming, so he kissed me quickly, and then he was gone.

I tried to act normal as my heart did summersaults in my chest. I just knew Karen was going to catch me with Kurt in the overgrown backyard, but she didn't. I was confused—flying the high of our kiss while also dealing with the intense feelings associated with knowing this would be the last time I set foot in my father's home.

Once the house sold, my dad accumulated money. He needed to spend a certain amount, his assets falling below a predetermined cutoff, to qualify for state medical insurance.

"You should try out for the cheerleading squad," Karen said to me one evening as we sat down to dinner. "We have to spend the money anyway, so you might as well get something out of it."

I agreed to try out, although I was unsure at first. By the second week of tryouts, I was all-in. I practiced my routines in the backyard. I stretched to improve my jumps and my kicks. Cheerleading distracted me from the constant worrying about my dad's illness. I was thrilled to be part of a team of girls who wanted me there.

"Do you really think you're going to have enough time to spend with your dad if you're going to practice five times a week?" Karen asked.

After I made the squad, Karen told me I needed to quit because being on the team wouldn't allow me enough time to visit my dad in the convalescent home.

I was speechless and heartbroken, knowing there was no argument to be had with her. She wasn't really asking me a question. She was telling me. I was quitting the cheerleading squad.

⊚ ⊚ ⊚

Karen and her family didn't like my long, curly hair. They claimed it got caught in the towels. Karen insisted I cut off my locks. I looked ridiculous with short hair. I was mortified when my peers would call me cruel names. I spent all of ninth grade walking around wearing a ski parka with the hood up. No matter how hot the day, I could be found with my Starter jacket on and my head fully covered.

After four months, I told Karen I was moving out and going to live with Amy. In preparation, I washed a load of laundry the day before I left. Karen wanted to put her clothes, which were wet from the washing machine, into the dryer. She called me over to check my clothes, which occupied the dryer at the time.

"They aren't dry yet," I told her.

Karen looked me right in the eye and said, "You're a bitch," then walked away.

I was caught completely off guard. Perhaps she was angry about my leaving. Maybe she thought me ungrateful for all she had done for me. I'll never know. My face flushed red, and I stood, shocked by her for the last time.

I was living at Amy's house for about three months when I discovered Amy's sister was using drugs. I made the decision to move out of their house.

The third house I lived in belonged to a family who worshipped at the church I started attending since my father fell ill. I met and became friends with their daughter, Colleen, who was in my class. The youth pastor was aware of my living situation, and he asked Colleen's parents if they would consider taking me in.

Colleen's parents criticized me for spending so much time in my bedroom. I kept to myself because, as an only child, this was what I was used to. I worried about my father night and day. I spent much of my free time visiting with him. This made me unavailable for other activities.

One evening, I was summoned for a conversation with the mother and father of the house. They quizzed me about how I was feeling regarding living with them. I told them I had moved around so much the last few months, I didn't really feel as though I "missed" anybody anymore.

The couple announced that they were going to pay for my church summer camp. I was very excited. I thanked them with honest enthusiasm and had a wonderful week at camp.

When I returned home, I told the woman of the house I had missed her. The look on her face signified that something was very wrong. Later the same evening, the couple sat me down and explained that I could no longer live with them. I was completely in shock. The next day, they took me to a county-run group home and left me there.

I was once again terrified. These were rough kids. This was a place for kids who were in trouble and/or court ordered to be there. I had no privileges. I had to earn the right to go outside for a walk.

"Your hair is cool," a resident said to me as I was still having the point system explained. "I'm going to braid it for you tonight."

I said nothing. I felt I wasn't in a position to argue. Later, I sat stiff on the floor while this girl I had just met braided my hair.

It must have been clear to the staff that I did not belong. A few days later, they moved me to another living situation.

The second group home had less restrictions, but I still didn't feel like I could relate to the other residents. The home was run by a mother and father. When the offer came to move to Helga's house, I accepted it. In hindsight, I should not have.

The offer came through a nurse at the convalescent home where my father lived. She had become aware of my situation. She knew Helga because her kids played on a sports team with Helga's son. Out of kindness, this nurse connected the dots, and my father gave his permission for me to stay with Helga.

The move to Helga's home included a change of high schools right in the middle of my sophomore year. I lost my social support system and had to navigate the new environment while dealing with difficult days in Helga's home.

The first two years I lived at Helga's house, my dad would call in the evenings from the convalescent home where he lived to say good night to me. He would hang up the phone and immediately call back again to say the exact same thing. He either forgot he called or was so lonely and bored that he couldn't help calling again.

I used to get so frustrated at these repetitive phone calls. Helga told me to stay by the phone to answer the calls. This went on, one after the other, night after night.

I hated myself for how angry I got at my dad. I tried to explain without hurting his feelings that he had just called, and he would promise not to call again, but then he would.

Years later, after my dad passed away, I would long for just one more phone call, just one more chance to hear him say, "I love you, pumpkin."

# CHAPTER FOUR

# Foster Mother

Helga and her husband had collected foster children from the three surrounding counties. The money they received monthly for caring for these children appeared to be their only source of income. Helga's husband sat in his chair, watching television, while the chaos swirled around him. There was a total of nine children when I lived in their house, not counting me or their two biological children.

I witnessed Helga physically abuse several of the children in her care. Depending on her mood, Helga hit and slapped children on a whim. The physical punishment was handed out erratically, so the children never knew when to expect it. One eleven-year-old boy with blue eyes and his two sisters, ages nine and thirteen, were fully adopted by Helga and her husband. He worked so hard for Helga's approval. If the blue-eyed boy didn't do exactly what Helga wanted, she would grab him by his big ears and yank him around. Two girls in the house, one of the blue-eyed boy's sisters and a twelve-year-old girl, were in charge of caring for a two-year-old, Susie, who was extremely hyperactive. Helga would ask for Susie to be brought to her for ten minutes, then return her to the girls to be supervised by them once again.

Much of the time, Helga did not allow six of these school-aged children to attend traditional school because she wanted them at home, working for her. I overheard her tell other adults she was homeschooling them. There were lessons once every month or so, but it was never consistent.

Some may wonder why I didn't tell someone about the living conditions or the abuse I witnessed while living in Helga's home. There was no one who would listen. Since my dad had given his permission for me to stay with Helga, I didn't have an assigned social worker. No one came to the house to check on me or make sure I was safe or properly cared for. I had some sense that I could contact child protective services (CPS), but I had no idea what the phone number was.

The kids didn't like the living conditions. They were too afraid of Helga to report her to their social worker. If a social worker assigned to a child came to the house, the kids would scurry around like ants cleaning things up and pretending everything was fine. Sometimes, social workers would show up unannounced, and we'd hide, hoping they'd leave, and after no answer at the door, they would. After all these years, I still carry guilt. Maybe there was something I could've done to stop Helga.

The house was disgustingly dirty. The floors were perpetually covered with dirt dragged in from outside. The dishes in the sink sat so long, collecting a putrid smell. The children assigned to wash the dishes had to use laundry detergent, as no dish soap was available. The walls were dirty with fingerprints. Children dug through piles of dirty clothes to find something to wear. Many of the clothes went through the washing machine and never made it to the dryer. Piles of sour, molding clothes crowded the living room, smelling like nothing I had ever smelled before.

Helga used money she received for my care to finance a week-long a trip to Disneyland for the entire household. Upon our return, I walked into Helga's kitchen to find maggots crawling on the dishes in the sink. There were baby bottles with curdled milk and so many plates and cups—the mess overflowed from the sink and onto the adjacent countertop. On every surface of those dishes crawled little white wriggling maggots. The smell was so foul, I began to dry heave. After reviewing the scene, Helga said, "Oh, shit, now we have to buy new bottles for the baby."

We never had sufficient food in the house. A common snack was a tortilla smeared with butter because there was no cheese. When I tried to make my lunch for school, there was no bread to be found. Fresh fruit was absent most of the time. The only vegetables in the house were canned.

Beyond any of these things, the worst part for me involved manipulation. My dad gave permission for Helga to be my guardian. As a ward of the state, a court-appointed guardian took charge of my finances. A $25 check arrived for me each week from my dad, and each time they did, Helga insisted I sign the checks over to her. To pacify me, Helga told me if I cleaned the entire house every day, I could earn the $25 per week. I cleaned, but there was no money forthcoming. I eventually gave up on the losing battle.

There were bigger monetary manipulations. For example, Helga told me to tell the court-appointed guardian that the car, which was bought with my dad's money, needed new brakes. It was rare for me to drive the car, which was driven almost exclusively by Helga's biological children. I could not argue with Helga, who would then find additional ways to make my life more of a living hell. The check would come in the mail, and I would sign it over to Helga so she could go to bingo or Walmart.

My six-by-ten-foot room included a window and a door. Three pieces of Sheetrock partitioned space for me in the barn. Another difficult thing about living at Helga's was hearing those dreaded footsteps, the ones coming to tell me I had to babysit the other nine non-biological children. One of the kids would be sent out to knock on my door and tell me, "Mom says you have to babysit." I hated those words.

Babysitting the younger kids was like juggling knives while

running a marathon. I held my breath in anticipation of what bad thing was going to happen. When the two-year-old hit her head hard on the coffee table—the sound like that of a ripe watermelon smashing to the ground—I was terrified. I held Susie's head in my hands while she screamed bloody murder for two hours until Helga got home. I had no idea what else to do. Calling 911 would result in Helga's rage. Health insurance was a luxury no one in Helga's home enjoyed, so far as I knew. I didn't want to have to pay a huge hospital bill myself. I wrapped my hands tightly around the child's skull, watching for signs of shock, fearing her head might come apart at any moment. When Helga got home, she got the child to stop crying and eventually put her to bed. Susie seemed fine the next morning.

◉ ◉ ◉

In spite of my pleas to go to school, I was sometimes kept home to babysit for Helga. School was my refuge, and being kept home made me feel small and demoralized. School was the one thing which kept my mind off my dad being sick in a convalescent home.

If I didn't do what Helga wanted, she punished me by not allowing me to visit my father.

Nothing that happened during the time I lived with Helga felt fair or safe. I couldn't have a normal emotional reaction to anything without being called a "storm cloud." I had lost the one basic human right, the right to my own feelings.

For the entire three years I lived with Helga, I told myself every day, "This has to end eventually." I tried to picture the day in my mind. I tried to imagine how I would feel to be free. This is what kept me going. This is what made life worth living during this very, very dark time.

Helga's biological daughter, Justine, who was two years older than me, was the one person who saw it all. She knew Helga's treatment was cruel. She knew once I left, there would be no coming back. Toward the end of my stay at Helga's home, Justine got me out of the house as often as possible. She became a lifeline for me. I know I can never fully repay her for her kindness.

# CHAPTER FIVE

# A Tale of Two Mothers

The memories I have of Deirdre are somewhat scattered. I remember the house on Rumble Road in Modesto, California. My earliest memory is stepping on a sticker weed barefoot in the front yard when I was three years old. My half-brother Liam taught me how to taste the honeysuckle in the backyard. He was twelve years my senior. He showed me how to gently pull away the petals so that only the center of the flower remained. The drop of sweet nectar was always so mesmerizing to me.

I remember when my maternal grandmother, Kate, fell down an escalator at the mall. Deirdre, Liam, Kate, and I were riding down an escalator. We had no sooner stepped on than Kate lost her footing and fell. Deirdre, Liam, and I watched in horror as she tumbled down the entire length of the escalator, doing summersaults as she went. As we reached the bottom of the escalator, mall security responded, and my half-brother took me outside. A few minutes later, police sirens could be heard, and several police cars stopped in front of the mall. When I finally saw my grandmother again, she had a terrible bump above her right eye. Deirdre helped Kate walk to the car. I was fearful of escalators for some time after this incident.

I remember how I got one of the many scars on my knees, falling on a screw sticking out of the carpet. I tore my blue onesie and the skin underneath it.

◎ ◎ ◎

I don't have any recent memories with Deirdre. As these words are being written, it has been approximately five years since I have spoken to Deirdre. There have been many attempts to rekindle contact with Deirdre since she lost custody of me. The first time was when I was sixteen years old. With my father in a convalescent hospital and no other family to turn to, I was wondering where on this earth I belonged. Reaching for someone to hold onto, I found Deirdre.

An early meeting took place at Helga's home. It may seem obvious, but I was nervous prior to the meeting. I experienced the kind of anxiety typically reserved for when one is being stalked by a lion. I had nervous butterflies in my stomach—and not in a good way—thinking, *There's nothing I can do about this except try to survive*. It was a sick energy that engulfed me.

Helga's behavior in Deirdre's presence was confusing for me. Helga was on her best behavior for the occasion. She spoke in a sickeningly sweet tone all night about what a great kid I was, which was an odd change of pace from the constant ridicule I was used to.

The two women fell instantly into step. Helga would tell a story about my awesome grades, and Deirdre would return the volley with a story about something brilliant I did as a baby. The two women danced in circles around me the entire night. The rest of the children in the room sat in awe.

As she began a story about my childhood, Deirdre touched my back, and my skin crawled. I didn't know whether my reaction was because Deirdre's touch was unexpected or if my body was reacting to something more sinister. But I knew something was not right.

The relationship forged ahead, mostly at the urging of Helga. In my opinion, this was because she thought she too would benefit from Deirdre's willingness to spend money freely. This was during my senior year of high school, and Deirdre paid for my senior pictures, my letterman jacket for swimming, and my driver's training.

I appreciated Deirdre's efforts to care about and support what was important to me. Deirdre also acted as though she adored me—a feeling I was no longer used to. In her eyes, I could do no wrong. As a sixteen-year-old girl, this attention felt like heaven compared to the hell I was living in.

Deirdre was not a wealthy woman, per se. I was told much later in life by a cousin who knew her well that Deidre took great care to marry well after her divorce from my father.

It was almost as if Deirdre made a show of spending money. Every restaurant had to be the fanciest. The clothing Deirdre wanted to buy for me had to be name-brand. Every gift had to be the most expensive.

I always thought her spending was overcompensation. I now realize there was more to it. Once there was no more money to be spent for the day, it was almost as if Deirdre wanted me out of her sight. She became insistent about her alone time. I had nothing to say about it. Looking back, it still doesn't make sense to me. The only thing I can say for certain—the one constant in my relationship with Deirdre was how confusing it always was for me.

The conversation didn't get too deep. We rarely approached the topic of my dad. Even more seldom did we discuss the topic of the allegations of abuse. When these things did come up, they were handled very carefully and mostly swept under the rug.

It wasn't long before I wanted to move in with Deirdre. Anything was better than being a live-in babysitter at Helga's home. I allowed myself to be wooed by Deirdre's gifts and money. While I did have some notion of disloyalty to my father, I longed for some normalcy in my life. I wanted to live with one of my parents. I wanted to have a relationship with Deirdre after so many years. I also knew this would make Deirdre very happy. To me, this was the right course of action for everyone involved, with the exception of Helga, who simply wasn't my priority.

Helga saw red. She knew if I moved out, she would no longer be able to manipulate me out of my estate money. Helga began to sow hate and discontent in the relationship between Deirdre and me. Helga complained about how unfair it was that I had nice things while she couldn't afford to buy similar things for the other children. She would get on the phone with Deirdre and make similar complaints, maybe expecting Deirdre to start buying things for all twelve kids in the house.

When Deirdre didn't comply, Helga simply got angrier and more bitter. Before long, Deirdre and Helga had an argument, and Deirdre was unable to stand up to Helga, disappearing from my life. In general, Deirdre is uncomfortable with discord of any kind. Although she probably could have gone to court, presented her case, and gained custody of me, I don't think she had the psychological strength to do so. As a result, I was left to fend for myself with Helga once again. Helga grounded me for a month in response to my efforts to move in with Deirdre.

# CHAPTER SIX

# Goodbye

My dad lived for about four years after the stroke, just as his first doctor had predicted.

As a sixteen-year-old junior, I wanted to participate in the traditional powderpuff football game. As an underclassman, I had anticipated the day when I could sign up for the festivities. During this game, the junior and senior girls played each other in football, while the junior and senior guys did the cheerleading on the sidelines for their respective teams. There were a few practices beforehand to prepare for the main event. I was already on the swim team, and any chance to be away from Helga's house was very attractive.

I remember it vividly—a Thursday afternoon, I had just arrived home after practice, and the phone was ringing. The convalescent hospital was calling.

"I think you should get here right away," said the concerned doctor on the other end of the line.

"Why?" I asked. "What's going on?"

"It seems as though your father has developed a bleeding ulcer. He's being transported to the emergency room at VacaValley Hospital now."

"A bleeding ulcer?" I was still confused. "Is that very serious?"

"Ma'am, I think you should get here as soon as possible."

His tone of voice told me what I needed to know.

Although Helga's house was typically well populated, no one else was home on this particular Thursday afternoon. There was no one to turn to. I called Gabe, the boy I was dating, and he gave me a ride to the convalescent hospital. I met the ambulance at the front doors of the convalescent home. I got into the ambulance briefly and said, "Daddy, I love you."

"I love you too," he answered me. He seemed alert and oriented, so I stepped back outside and asked the EMT, "Is my dad going to be alright?"

The young man just shook his head and said, "If only we had gotten to him sooner." He closed the ambulance doors and walked briskly away from me.

In hindsight, I should have been panicking right then, but I wasn't. I kept the panic at bay by telling myself how my dad seemed fine, and how he was going to be fine.

Gabe and I got back into his car and followed the ambulance the few blocks to the hospital emergency room. I went into the ER and took my dad's hand in my own.

"Can I have a cigarette?" he asked.

A wave of frustration washed over me, and I quickly fought it back. "No, Dad, you can't smoke in here."

"Then take me outside," he said, his voice almost demanding.

"No, Dad, not right now," I told him. My heart felt sick. Here my dad was, lying on a gurney, fighting for his life, his mind occupied with smoking another cigarette.

Just then, I was called away by a nurse to fill out some insurance paperwork. As I started to walk away, my dad grabbed my hand, pulled me back toward him, and whispered, "I love you."

"I love you too, Dad." Those were the last words I ever spoke to my father.

I finished the paperwork and was escorted to the waiting room. A few minutes later, a nurse came in and told me my dad's heart had stopped, and they had performed CPR to resuscitate him. One of my dad's nurses summoned me from the ER waiting area back to say my final goodbyes. By the time I got to the doors of the emergency room, two other nurses stood, blocking my path. One of them said, "I'm sorry, he's gone."

In shock, I vaguely remember being led back to a small private room, sobbing. Gabe waited there, as did his father, who was a pastor at the church we attended. Gabe stayed in the ER waiting area, and his dad was called by the hospital to give my father last rites.

I was awash with grief. No amount of role-playing came close to preparing me for what I felt in that moment. There was no way to imagine how lost, alone, and abandoned I would feel. My daddy was gone. Nothing would ever be the same.

Helga arrived at some point. She offered little emotional support. She took me to gather my father's things from the convalescent hospital. I held his blue suitcase in one hand and a large rainbow kite in the other. The kite represented my life with my father before he got sick. I remember the joy of flying kites with him in the summer sun. Walking out of the convalescent hospital, a nurse stopped me and asked, "Is your dad going home?"

I wanted to scream at her. I wanted to unleash all the pain and anger inside of me. Instead, I paused, thought for a moment, and simply responded, "Yes, my dad is going home."

The weeks following my dad's passing were unbearable. As I was grieving the death of my father, one of Helga's foster kids asked me if I thought my dad had gone to heaven or hell. Floored, I looked at the child and told her this wasn't an appropriate question to ask someone who just lost a loved one. The child answered immediately, saying her mom had told her she could ask me whatever she wanted about my dad. This was one of the few times I defied Helga outright. I looked at the child squarely and said, "I really don't care what your mom says. Don't ask me that again."

Later, a review of my father's medical records and interviews with the staff at the convalescent hospital would reveal he had a bleeding ulcer for some time before it took his life. His symptoms—overlooked during medical rounds and routine bathroom trips—could have saved his life if the staff had followed normal procedure.

Helga was the catalyst for a wrongful death lawsuit brought against the convalescent hospital where my dad had lived. The owners of the place settled out of court for a minimal amount. The lawyer involved took the money and set up an annuity in my name, so Helga never saw a penny of it.

My dad and I at the Japanese tea Garden in San Francisco.

# CHAPTER SEVEN

# The Moment of Recall

As part of the court ordered forensic evaluation, Dr. David Corwin recorded several video interviews of me as a young child. One interview took place after I was brought in by my father and Agnes. In this video, I am happy and confident. Another happened after I had been transported by Deirdre and her mother. Although the content in the interview is the same, I appear uncomfortable and whiny. One of my first questions is, "Can they hear me from the waiting room?" When Dr. Corwin assures me they cannot, I recount the same story I told when my dad and Agnes brought me in for the first interview. This retelling includes Deirdre putting her fingers in my vagina while she is bathing me as a young child. A third interview was conducted just before Dr. Corwin testified with his findings. Only Dr. Corwin and I appeared in the third video. During this interview, my demeanor is much more matter of fact, and the content is much more businesslike.

Over the years, Dr. Corwin contacted my father and me to get permission to use the video recordings in professional presentations. Mental health professionals used videos like mine to train custody evaluators on how to talk to children. My privacy was important to Dr. Corwin, and he always excluded my name and protected my identity. Neither my father nor I ever anticipated any negative fallout should my true identify become known.

When asked, I had always given Dr. Corwin my assent. I wanted to help other traumatized children as much as possible.

At the time, I believed that allowing Dr. Corwin to use the videos accomplished this goal in some small way.

I also wanted to be a child psychologist someday. Working with Dr. Corwin as a young child, I remembered him as the only person who wanted to hear what I had to say without adding his own agenda. I wanted to provide the same experience to other children who went through difficult experiences.

When I was sixteen, a few months before my father passed away, I was feeling lost and anchorless, confused and uncertain. That's when Dr. Corwin contacted me about my videos. I asked him if I could watch them, trying to understand what happened to me. At the time, I did not recall the allegations of sexual abuse I made against Deirdre.

Dr. Corwin hesitated and eventually asked me if I could wait until he could be present with me and ensure my emotional well-being. I agreed, and it was about a year later that we watched them.

I felt both curious and nervous. Dr. Corwin's presence made me feel safe. He interviewed me before and after watching the videos. I was excited to get answers to some long unanswered questions I had about my life. *Why was Deirdre not in my life when I was a young child? Why did Deidre lose custody of me? What happened?*

Prior to watching the videos of myself as a five-year-old, Dr. Corwin, once again video recording our conversation, asked me if I remembered anything about alleged sexual abuse. I immediately said no. I paused, then commented that something felt "really weird." I began to talk about an incident of abuse at Deirdre's hand. This is the point at which I recovered the memory. I told Dr. Corwin that it was like my mind took a "snapshot of the pain." Later, I was unsure whether the pain had been inflicted intentionally or by accident. This was—according to Dr. Corwin and others—the first time an individual had been video recorded while experiencing the return of a memory of abuse.

After this recall incident, Dr. Corwin and I watched the original videos together. I was struck by how sure of myself I seemed at such a young age. I told the story with conviction despite admonishments from Dr. Corwin to "tell the truth now." As a child, I was very spontaneous in the way I talked about the events. I do not believe I was coached into saying the things I said. To me, it seemed as though the little girl on the videos was telling the truth.

In one of the interviews, Dr. Corwin asked me a series of math questions. He told me the answer to one question, then asked me if I knew the answer before he told me. I simply responded, "no," without any attempt to cover up my lack of knowledge. His purpose was to ensure I was not answering in the affirmative in an effort to please the adult in the room. He wanted to show future watchers of the video that I wasn't just saying yes to every question he asked me.

I tell of the events in Deirdre's bathtub with a great deal of conviction. I am able to repeat details reliably over time. The narrative does not seem rehearsed or forced. I follow the conversation about where the abuse took place, in Deidre's house, in the bathroom. I respond to challenges of my story with the willfulness of a much older child.

The day I recalled the memory, I left Dr. Corwin's office feeling confident I knew the truth of what happened to me. I felt my memory was real and accurate. I gained new knowledge of my own past—something that felt both refreshing and nightmarish. While that feeling was empowering, it was also a terrifying discovery.

# CHAPTER EIGHT

# In the Navy

After my dad died, school continued to be my safe place. Continuing my high school studies, I felt isolated while I worked through my grief.

I graduated high school with almost all As. I took the SAT on a whim and qualified to go directly to college. Helga made me believe my only choices were to join the military or go to the local junior college. I doubt she ever thought I would actually join the military. Her ultimatum made my choice very easy. My dad had joined the Navy right out of high school, and if it was good enough for him, it was good enough for me. I began to prepare myself both physically and mentally. I took the Armed Services Vocational Aptitude Battery (ASVAB) and qualified for the Nuclear Power School (NPS) training program.

Helga likely presented the military as the most undesirable option because her goal was to get me to stay. She probably wanted me to attend the local junior college so I could keep being her live-in babysitter and she could still access my father's inheritance.

I contacted Deirdre in an effort to gain her consent to join the Navy before I turned eighteen. She refused. Legally, there was no one else to ask.

After graduation, I worked as a lifeguard for the two and half months until I turned eighteen. Three days after my birthday, I enlisted in the Navy. I never returned to Helga's home.

I felt somewhat conflicted about leaving Helga's home. I knew this was my only chance to get out and make a clean break.

Leaving those other kids behind was hard. It came to light later that some of them were angry at me, which made the pain and guilt of leaving all the more real.

A few years after joining the Navy, while I was visiting my hometown, I made a stop at Walmart. Helga spotted me at the checkout stand. She sent the boy with blue eyes to ask me, "How do you live with yourself knowing you are everything you are because of her?" This comment—coming from him, no less—broke my heart. Far enough removed from the poison of Helga's house by then, I sensed that this was one of many lies she told the other kids about me. Without even thinking, I looked the blue-eyed boy right in the eyes and told him, "I'm everything I am in spite of her, not because of her," and walked out of the store.

Decades after the Walmart incident, the blue-eyed boy and I are now close. I try to keep up with what is going on with the rest of the children from Helga's home without invading their lives too much.

The blue-eyed boy and I have decided not to maintain a relationship with Helga because it's impossible to set boundaries with her or keep her chaos from spilling into the lives around her. Despite Helga's attempts to contact me via social media, I simply leave that bridge unrepaired, for better or worse.

I went to basic training in Great Lakes, Illinois. Boot camp was scary, although I was prepared well for the challenge. The running and physical training rarely became more than I could handle. I often enjoyed the comradery of exercising with my division. The academics were straightforward, and my leadership role included helping other recruits prepare for the tests. Although I found the marching mundane, it also made me feel proud to be a part of such a long-standing tradition. The scariest part had to be all the yelling. I was also terrified they would cut off my long curly hair. I got up early every day and made sure my hair was perfect. I gave the division commanders no reason to consider sending me for a haircut. My hair and I made it through basic training without incident.

The toughness of basic training was pleasant in comparison to the chaos at Helga's. The rules were consistent, and the consequences predictable.

One afternoon, I was sitting in a classroom with my entire division when a man walked in and asked for everyone's attention. He asked the members of the group to raise their hands if they had taken the SAT. I raised my hand. He asked those with hands up to keep them up if they had earned over a specific score on the SAT. I kept my hand up. He again asked those with hands up to keep their hands up if they had earned a 3.5 or higher GPA in high school. I looked around and realized I was the only recruit with my hand up. The man walked down the aisle and handed me a packet of papers, then turned and walked out of the room.

Without knowing it, I had just qualified myself for an interview with the Naval Reserve Officer Training Corps (NROTC) program. I spent the next few weeks calling and gathering letters of recommendation and high-school transcripts. I attended an interview, during which I felt so nervous that I still cannot recall the content of it to this day. I continued on with basic training and did not think much about the application or the interview for several months.

I made it through basic training and reported to Orlando, Florida, for nuclear power training. I was assigned the role of Machinist's Mate, the mechanics of the Navy, Third Class. I started Machinist's Mate A School and knew pretty much right away that I was a poor fit for this position. I was not mechanical at all, and I was not terribly interested in learning how to be mechanical.

One afternoon, I was walking past a pay phone when I thought of the NROTC interview I had done almost eight months before. On a whim, I dialed 1-800-USA-NAVY and waited to speak to an operator. This was another of those moments which changed everything for me. The voice on the other end of the line told me I had been selected for an NROTC scholarship.

This meant four years of college—paid for. In addition, I had been selected to be an officer in the United States Navy. I stood there, holding the phone, first stunned, then elated.

I thanked the woman on the other end of the telephone line. I found my section leader and told him the good news. I asked him to keep this information to himself. I was afraid of the jealous reaction other students might have.

A few weeks later, I attended a class about how to clean strainers. As the class leader, I usually didn't have to get too dirty during labs. But on this day, the class was instructed by a chief who ensured I ended up elbow deep in the strainer, my entire arm covered in lube oil. I had not expected this. The chief asked me if I knew why. I was so mad, I answered him through my teeth. When I told him I had no idea, he looked me dead in the eye and told me I was never to forget where I came from, and then announced to the class that I had been selected for an officer training program.

It would be several months before I would be released from my enlisted contract and accept the scholarship to attend the University of San Diego. Until then, I had to continue nuclear training. Unlike high school, I studied concepts which were foreign to me. I started to panic when a test didn't go well or when I didn't know the answer to a question. I found this frustrating. I started to overthink things. This would be the first of several times I almost allowed insecurity to get in my way.

When I got my orders to San Diego and knew for sure I wouldn't be finishing nuclear power school, I started to do well on exams again. The pressure had been taken off, I had relaxed a little, and everything fell back into place.

# CHAPTER NINE

# The Case Report

Based on my previous experience giving assent to Dr. Corwin to use the videos of me as a small child for training purposes, I believe there was some pattern in place. It seemed normal to me to allow him to use my material for his training purposes. Yet now, as a psychologist, I'm very aware of the power that mental health professionals often have over their patients, and the difficulty participants may have saying no, even if they want to. I didn't give it much thought back then. I never considered the possible ramifications. I was a young child when I initially gave Dr. Corwin permission to use the videos and only seventeen when he recorded my spontaneous memory recall.

Dr. Corwin was on the editorial board of *Child Maltreatment*, a peer-reviewed journal in psychology. During a board meeting, the editor, Mark Chaffin, asked the members of the editorial board for ideas to fill spots in the upcoming issue. Dr. Corwin told me he hesitated to mention my case report, but on an impulse, he brought up our interview and my "spontaneous recollection."

Dr. Corwin will tell you he had no intention of becoming a part of the so-called "memory wars" by writing about what happened in the room with me that day. He simply thought it was interesting.

It was several months after I finished basic training when Dr. Corwin and I spoke again. He told me there were no case studies in which memory recall had been captured on video. He explained traumatic event memory recall could not be "staged" for ethical reasons. He asked for my permission to distribute the video to several experts in the field to obtain some commentary. The collective analysis would then be published as a case report. I agreed, allowing the case report to move forward. I always agreed to Dr. Corwin's requests. I wanted to help other children who had trauma like mine. Little did I know—this one decision would change my life in such a dramatic way.

Having joined the Navy, I gave my consent and forgot about the case report. I had so much going on in my life, there was no room in my consciousness for the past. I concentrated on moving forward. Self-reflection wasn't on my mind—my future was.

Forward movement was important for me for other reasons too. While my peers had the luxury of a financial and emotional safety net, I was not afforded such extravagance. I had no one to borrow money from if I came up short on my bills at the end of the month. While I did have some friends from back home, I was starkly aware of how alone I was in the world. I had no real ties to anyone.

Participating in the case report reconnected me to a world that I previously felt alienated from. I owned my experiences, and I was able to share them and help others. Something remarkable had happened to me, and I had the opportunity to turn it into a learning experience for the mental health field. I felt I was about to make a solid contribution.

My connections to the world had asterisks. I have a biological mother, but we are estranged. I have a father, but he is deceased. This contribution to psychology was pure. There was no asterisk and no need for extra explanation.

# CHAPTER TEN

# The Intrusion

College was difficult for me socially. Nothing in my recent past had prepared me to create adult friendships, set appropriate boundaries, or build appropriate attachments to others. I had been through military training, and my priorities were slightly different than the average college freshman. I had been forced to grow up— both by my life circumstances and military training—and I found it difficult to return to my previous civilian perceptions of the world. In the military, I was used to thinking in ordered steps; as a civilian, order is often looked down upon.

In addition to the social challenges, I had financial challenges. I gave up the steady paycheck from the military to go to college. I had a small monthly stipend, whatever was left after college expenses each semester, and a part-time job as a lifeguard at the local YMCA. My life experience was hardly comparable to students who had just left their parents' house with the safety net of returning any time.

My roommate situation was also difficult and exhausting. The suite contained four bedrooms, a living room, and two bathrooms, with two girls per bedroom. Our suite was separated from the main campus by a large hill. While many of my roommates made the climb up to campus to eat at the cafeteria, I typically ate off campus. There was no shortage of fast-food restaurants nearby. Before I left USD, the Domino's Pizza right off campus made a deal with the university, allowing students to use their campus cash cards to pay for pizza.

The girl I shared a room with was sixteen years old. She had the mentality of a young teenager, and very little life experience. She got caught driving under the influence the first month of school, and not only did she need rides to and from her Alcoholics Anonymous meetings, but she needed rides everywhere. She also had a boyfriend who was in his twenties. My roommate and I did not get along so well.

Once, the other seven roommates decided it would be a good idea to try mushrooms. The threat of drug tests looming over my head, that was not an option for me. (I wasn't actually asked to submit a drug test until I returned to active duty.) There was a huge, undeveloped canyon near the dorm. I could hear my roommates howling—just like the wild coyotes did at night—running through the canyon while I studied for my midterms.

Being in a classroom felt as close to home as possible for me. I was once again in my safe space, thriving. The struggle with my female roommates would not be a one-time occurrence. I struggled with friendships, especially with females, for decades beyond college.

College life was moderately predictable until a message on my pager interrupted the calmness, reigniting a fear in me that was also all too familiar. It was 1997, at which point cell phones were still uncommon, although the pager was ubiquitous.

"911," it read. I stood there, stunned, fixated on my pager. It took a few moments before I was able to shake off my surprise and blink again. The page was from a good friend back home who I would often stay with when I was back in my hometown.

Before this page came in, I was off campus at a party, an apartment-style dorm room, loud, smoky, and crowded. As the music blared, people leaned in close to each other to have conversations despite the noise. I was on a balcony talking to a cute guy I had just met.

I was a nineteen-year-old freshman at the University of San

Diego. This was the only party my roommates had invited me to—leaving to find a phone would destroy what was left of my social reputation.

I weighed my options, but I ended up waiting until the following morning to return the page. When I did, I found out that my friend and her family were contacted by a private investigator who was looking for me. I instantly started to shake. "A private investigator?" I asked, "Are you sure?"

I hung up the phone and sat for a while, unsure what to do. Why on earth would anyone be looking for me? Whatever the reason, I had a bad feeling about it. It felt as though something was trying to gnaw through my stomach from the inside.

I suddenly realized this had to relate to Dr. Corwin's published case report. That had to be the reason. There was nothing else I could think of that would warrant such interest. I knew I needed to reach out to Dr. Corwin. Hopefully he could help me figure this out.

# CHAPTER ELEVEN

# The Memory Researcher

When I did connect with Dr. Corwin—filling him in on the private investigator and how distressed I was—he said he would look into it and let me know what he found out.

A few days later, Dr. Corwin told me he figured out who the private investigator was working with—Dr. Malvonia East.

Dr. East is a memory researcher. She has made her living, at least in part, by testifying as an expert witness. She testifies almost exclusively for the defense in cases involving repressed memories. Dr. East was questioned on the witness stand about the Jane Doe case report. This is the case report Dr. Corwin published involving me. Rather than contact Dr. Corwin and discuss it—scientist to scientist—Dr. East opted to uncover my identity and send a private investigator to unpack the details of my personal life.

At only nineteen years old, this felt like a very dangerous situation. Other young adults in this situation had family surrounding, supporting, and protecting them. I had no one. I was alone and vulnerable. I felt scared and exposed. A stranger was collecting private details about my life. I had no idea what to expect next.

Someone who would go to this trouble to find me was, in my opinion, capable of anything. I just wanted Dr. East to stop. I emailed her, asking her to discontinue her efforts to contact me and collect information about my life. Her response was clear— she wasn't going to stop.

A few weeks after I found out a private investigator was looking for me, I visited my hometown. I stayed with the friend who had paged me. My car was parked in front of their home. While I was out, the same private investigator paid another visit.

After he was told I was not home, he left his card and turned to leave. Then he paused, circled back around, and informed the person who had answered the door, "Nicole should have the air in her front left tire checked. It looks a little low."

When I received this message, a chill ran down my back. He knew my car, and he wanted me to know it. It is a creepy feeling to realize you've been watched without your knowledge. I felt violated, exposed, and confused. I wanted to run and hide somewhere. There was nowhere safe to hide now. My sense of control over my own life had been taken from me.

Panicked, I had no idea what to do next. At this point in my life, I was not an academic. I was not familiar with the Institutional Review Board (IRB), which I now know is a type of committee charged with applying research ethics by reviewing the methods proposed for research to ensure they are ethical. These boards are formally designated to approve, or reject, monitor, and review behavioral research involving humans.

Dr. East was collecting information about me and my past. I wondered what she was going to do with the information. Was she preparing to write an article? A series of articles? Would she make me the unwilling participant in yet another case report without even bothering to ask for my consent?

What I lacked in knowledge, I made up for in resolve. Dr. East was, at the time, affiliated with a prominent university in the Northwestern United States. The university had a supervising board called the Human Subjects Review Committee. I felt thrilled and relieved. The name said it all. I was a human, the subject of a case report, and felt I had been treated unethically by a member of their university. It seemed as though they had to help.

Suppose I had agreed to discuss some behavior that was

shameful for some reason. This is often what a psychologist asks of a subject in a case study. The confidentiality aspect of the case study is supposed to be sacrosanct. If the ultimate outcome in my case was the risk people were asked to shoulder, then I doubt anyone would agree to take part in a case study.

A case study is merely a *proof of concept*. It does not bear the burden of proof by statistical significance or replication as does a research study.

# CHAPTER TWELVE

# The Lawyer

Alan Scheflin, a lawyer and law professor, found out that I was targeted by Malvonia East. He had an association with various individuals who were interested in protecting targets of Malvonia East. Julian Hubbard was a former student of Mr. Scheflin, and he agreed to take my civil case pro bono.

While most of my peers stood outside the buildings on campus and chatted with friends, I had heated discussions with my attorney via cell phone. I distinctly remember standing on the green grass, trying to move as little as possible so as not to lose reception.

Julian bore the brunt of my anger during the months leading up to and during the trial. Even when I was at my worst, Julian was steadfast and patient. I have no idea why he put up with me. I ranted about the unfairness of it all, ignoring that Julian had nothing to do with the emotional injuries bestowed upon me. I also had difficulty absorbing what he was trying to explain to me— the law or the legal reasons we had to proceed in a specific way.

I recall standing in front of one of USD's immaculate buildings with stone statues and well-manicured lawns while screaming into my cell phone at Julian. Passersby must have thought I lost my mind. I didn't care. My singular goal in that moment was to have someone bear witness to my pain, and I found a captive audience in Julian. To think he never got paid for any of this, I feel I owe him an apology. To Julian, I say this: *I'm sorry. I wish I could go back and somehow give you back the time you spent trying to right what went so terribly wrong in my life. I wish I had the money to compensate for all you did for me. All I can say is I'm sorry. Thank you for everything you did—and for everything you continue to do for me.*

Around the time Julian agreed to take my case, I went to one of my psychology professors and told her what Dr. East had done. The professor said my story sounded similar to the famous memory patient, H.M. As cruel as it may sound, "Everyone was sort of waiting for him to die so they could cut open his brain and see what was going on in there." I did not want to hear this. Professor Jones was the first outside person I opened up to about my story, and her reaction was dismissive and cold—I just needed someone to care.

# CHAPTER THIRTEEN

# The Human Subjects
# Review Committee

When scientists disagree, it is common to either develop an experiment designed to disprove the theory or engage in scholarly discussions with other experts in the field. It is inappropriate to uncover the identity of the research participants and systematically interview them or their families.

In my case, Dr. East couldn't create an experiment that disproved the observations in the Jane Doe case report. If Dr. East created an experimental protocol in an attempt to prove her theory, it would never be approved by an institutional review board. The information gained would not justify the potential damage it could cause to the human subjects. It is the responsibility of the IRB to protect human subjects whenever possible.

The inability to create an experimental protocol does not justify Dr. East's actions in my case, which also happens to be my life. It would have been her choice whether to include Dr. Corwin. It is my opinion that she should have engaged in some dialogue with her fellow scientists. I feel his participation would have made the discussion more credible. To take the extreme action of hiring an investigator violated my privacy.

She contacted every living person to whom I had an emotional attachment. This included my biological mother, to whom Dr. East appeared a sympathetic ear after so many years. Dr. East also interviewed Helga, who later stated in court records that she was misled to believe Dr. East was Dr. Corwin's supervisor. Agnes was also contacted, although I am unsure of the context of this communication.

After I found out about being tracked by a private investigator, I contacted a man named John Slattery. He was the associate dean for academic programs and the director of the office of scholarly integrity. I explained the invasion of privacy and the impact it was having on my life. He was sympathetic and assured me he would look into the matter. The investigation went on without result for almost two years.

While the committee's investigation was ongoing, Dr. East was told by the committee to stop her investigation of me. This left me in purgatory, waiting for resolution. I tried to put it out of my mind. It is difficult to describe what Dr. East did to me. She inserted herself into my life and fumbled around, knocking over nineteen years of neatly stacked traumas not yet sorted, processed, or filed away, looking for what she wanted, then left me to deal with the scattered remnants of her intrusion.

I contacted the committee on several occasions, only to be told they were "very close" to making a decision. Finally, the Human Subjects Review Committee decided Dr. East shouldn't investigate me anymore. As a result of their findings, she was also required to take an ethics class.

Dr. East left her university in the Northwest and moved to another university in Southern California.

Once she relocated, Dr. East reinitiated her investigation of me. She later published two articles in a non-peer reviewed magazine. To me, her articles gave a roadmap of how she uncovered my identity.

Most scientific journals require a peer-review process. During this process, the article is sent to two or more qualified individuals in the field of study. Often times, the peer reviewers and the authors are intentionally kept anonymous in an effort to avoid conflicts of interest, reprisals, or censorship on the part of the reviewer. Once the reviewers make their comments, the article is sent back to the author for editing.

I cannot say for certain that Dr. East's articles would not have made it through a peer-review process, although it is my biased opinion that they would not have. I am also of the opinion that peer-reviewed articles generally offer more credibility. I have wondered if Dr. East's decision to publish in a magazine was intentional so she could later insist her work was *journalism*. By choosing a magazine, she avoided the ethical review of psychologists, which she claimed didn't apply.

# CHAPTER FOURTEEN

# First Husband

After getting out of the Navy to go to college, I was left with very little to hold onto. My dad was gone, Deirdre was not a steady presence in my life, and there were no siblings or other family. I felt like a plastic bag floating in the wind. I felt unanchored and adrift, and I needed something, or someone, to ground me. Steve turned out to be that person for a while.

I met my first husband, Steve, through a mutual friend as an undergrad at USD. We seemed to click, so we started dating. We were young, and our relationship was more like a babbling brook than a rushing river. I thought it was something that would last. My few female friends told me to "hold onto this guy," as they had never seen me so happy.

The only problem was, Steve was in the military, and by the time he proposed, he already had orders to Norfolk, Virginia. Ever the problem solver, I organized a wedding on a moment's notice. We were married at the Bahia Hotel in San Diego. I wore a white dress, having paid more than I should have for the extravagance. There were twelve people in attendance, and it rained the entire day. Steve left for Norfolk two days later while I stayed in San Diego to tie up a few more loose ends.

A week later, I made arrangements to change schools and packed up my car, heading East with my cat, Solo.

As soon as I got there, the arguing began. We argued over trivial things. Steve had a friend, Tammy, with whom he worked. Four days after I arrived, the three of us went out to dinner. While

I was driving, Tammy and I got into an argument. I stopped the car in the parking lot of the restaurant, and all three of us got out. I walked toward the building, and Steve and Tammy walked toward the park. I had all the information I needed when Steve followed his friend instead of me. There was more to it than the arguing. I felt smothered instead of comforted when Steve held me at night. He was immature in ways I did not find attractive or endearing. In the end, I was married to Steve for all of one year before we filed for a summary dissolution. I never felt good about the way things turned out with Steve or that I had a failed marriage. But I'll always have Steve to thank for being my anchor at a time when I needed one.

I put what I didn't need in storage and headed back to San Diego exactly one week after having arrived in Norfolk. My return to San Diego was seamless, and I carried on with classes and NROTC training as usual.

I felt grounded long enough to finish my final year of college. I was ready to move on to the next phase of my life.

# CHAPTER FIFTEEN

# The Articles

Having accepted an NROTC scholarship, I was committed to serving at least four years in the Navy as a commissioned officer after graduation. I had ended my marriage, dealt with Dr. East's efforts to investigate my private life, graduated from college, and been commissioned as an officer in the United States Navy. I was twenty-one years old and in flight school in Milton, Florida, by the time Dr. East's first article was published.

I had a flight school classmate named Katherine. She and I were learning to fly the T-37 helicopter. Katherine had been such a rockstar all throughout flight school. I was so close to being a failure, it was hard for me to imagine why Katherine wanted to be friends with me. I felt the same way about nearly all my relationships.

I received a call that caught me by complete surprise. It was brought to my attention that the first article had been published. I knew I couldn't face it alone, so I asked Katherine to go along for emotional support.

The town of Milton didn't have a major bookstore, so Katherine went with me to a Pensacola bookstore to purchase a copy of the magazine.

In her article, Dr. East asserted that it was Agnes, my former stepmother, who suggested that I was abused by Deirdre. Dr. East also talked about my father in this article. She claimed he had an alcohol problem. I don't recall ever seeing my dad drunk. Dr.

East had interviewed my maternal half-brother, Liam, then thirty-three, who is mentally disabled from a serious car accident when he was a teenager. She published his account of incidents in which my father supposedly physically abused him, but she failed to mention Liam's compromised memory from his traumatic brain injury. To my knowledge, Dr. East did not corroborate Liam's account of events prior to publishing the article.

Dr. East published her accusations against my father, but he never had the chance to defend himself. He had died years earlier. Dr. East also drew her conclusions about me without ever interviewing me. I would have liked the chance to tell my side of the story. It is incredibly unfair for a psychologist to publish opinions based on evidence collected from others with their own agendas. The unfairness of this was hurtful and frustrating, and I wanted to protect my father's reputation as well as my own. Initially, I didn't know what to do. I was enraged. I felt helpless to take effective action against Dr. East and these words no one could unpublish. Words, much like bullets, cannot be recalled once fired.

Regarding Dr. East's failure to contact me during her investigation of my case, I would have preferred an advance copy of a story about me and the people I loved so much. I would've then been able to correct hurtful and egregious inaccuracies before it was made public. Reading them may have been painful. Seeing my life interpreted by a hostile evaluator, published without my contribution, was more painful. I was never given the opportunity to work with her—the choice was made for me. When I was involved with a group that wrote a series of articles in response to Dr. East's "Jane Doe" articles, including mine, Dr. East was invited to comment before publication, and she chose not to respond.

Dr. East was defending her theory that there could be no accurate recovered memory of abuse. It was useful to her to present my father as the evil player, and mother as innocent, since this version of the story means my "recovered memory" was likely false.

Further violating my privacy, Dr. East gathered information to blacken my father's name. Up to this point, I had every reason to be proud of my role in this scenario. While I would never have chosen to make my story public, I shared with close friends that I was Jane Doe. Now anyone could read Dr. East's view of me as a disturbed young woman with an alcoholic father who had subjected her innocent mother to grief.

Deirdre talked to me about her relationship with Dr. East. It was clear to me from reading her article that Dr. East and Deirdre formed a relationship. She used the information she had gained from her interactions with Deirdre in her articles. For example, the accusation that my father was an alcoholic came directly from Deirdre.

Helga submitted a statement, later used in court, in which she asserted that Dr. East had claimed to be Dr. Corwin's supervisor, which was a clear misstatement of the facts. There was no professional or personal relationship between Dr's. East and Corwin whatsoever, as both now admit.

I sat quietly on a wooden bench in the bookstore, with Katherine sitting to my left. I must have been in shock. I felt very little. Maybe it hadn't quite sunk in. We sat in silence for ten minutes before I found my voice. "Let's go," I said, and without missing a beat, Katherine and I walked out of the bookstore.

It wasn't until later, when I was alone in my apartment, that I emotionally fell apart. I was finishing the dishes, an ordinary activity, but I was overcome with emotion. I ran to my bedroom, threw my body on my bed, and buried my face in my pillow. I sobbed for five minutes, then I was calm for two, then the sobbing started again. This went on for an hour before I could control my tears at last. I was absolutely disgusted, sickened, repulsed, and appalled. It really can't be stated strongly enough—I was devastated by her accusations. I felt as though my life story had been taken from me.

# CHAPTER SIXTEEN

# Flight School

I struggled with hand-eye coordination in flight school. The more I struggled, the more anxious I got, and the more anxious I got, the more I struggled. I came closer than I would like to admit to failing out of flight school before I realized I was sabotaging myself.

I volunteered to cross-train with the Air Force, knowing the odds of success were lower. The rumor was if a Navy student made it through training at Vance Air Force Base, then she was sure to get jets, which was the goal of almost every pilot going through flight training. Because the positions were so highly sought-after, only the students with the highest scores earned the right to claim the positions in the jet training pipeline. Normally, only the strongest Navy students made it through Air Force training, which meant they got their pick of aircraft as well.

Air Force training was hard. It felt like they played by different rules than the Navy did. Navy instructors wanted students to know about aircraft systems and how the aircraft worked while Air Force trainers only seemed interested in emergency procedures.

I stayed on a watchlist of students in need of special attention for most of my primary training. After three failed events (i.e., flight, simulator, exam) in flight school, a student was considered for attrition from the program. To support struggling students, the chain of command created a Commander's Awareness Program (CAP) to which a student was assigned after a single failed event.

Then there was the airsickness. I got airsick the first twelve times I went flying in flight school. They sent me to a chair, lovingly called the "spin and puke," literally a barstool with a guardrail around it, and the person from physiology would just sit there and spin the seated would-be pilot until—you guessed it—she threw up. While this humiliation was happening, the physiology officer would politely walk out of the room, leaving the poor puker on her own to endure both the suffering and the embarrassment of losing her breakfast into a small paper bag. I was convinced this was simply an attempt to punish the airsickness out of me rather than any effort to cure what ailed me.

The flight surgeon prescribed medication for my airsickness. The medication on its own made me sick.

In the end, I started to associate the smells of the parachute locker, the rubbing alcohol used to clean my mask, and the rubber smell of the mask itself with getting airsick. Once I overcame this association, I overcame my airsickness, at least for a while. Years later, my husband Gary took me on a flight over the Grand Canyon. I spent almost the entire flight puking, although what I did see of the scenery was amazing.

In addition to my anxiety and airsickness, the Air Force Captain who was in charge of me, Captain Henry, was taking steps to ensure I failed out of the program. During a somewhat casual conversation with another Air Force captain, Captain Roberts, I found out Captain Roberts had been given orders by Captain Henry to "fail that bitch out of my program."

My stubborn streak was instantly mobilized. I wasn't going to let some entitled Air Force officer decide my fate. My previous experience at Helga's house taught me not to expect kind treatment. Having survived Helga's house, I wasn't going to give up now. I laughed, finished my beer, excused myself, then went home to study.

I did some serious soul-searching and had some deep discussions with my classmates. I realized I was putting in less than my full effort. Subconsciously, this was my way of softening the blow of failure. If I hadn't given it my all, failing wouldn't embarrass me as much. If I gave it my all and still failed, that weight would sit heavier on my chest. I eventually realized I had two choices—keep doing what I was doing and fail or go all-out and have a chance at success.

I took that chance, and I did succeed.

After I finished Air Force training, I was assigned to train as a helicopter pilot. One of the first lessons when learning to fly helicopters is hovering the aircraft. I was all over the place. I had a death grip on the controls, and my inputs were so big, they caused the aircraft to sway too far one way, which then required another input in the other direction . . . and so on.

One of my instructors took me out to a ten-foot, square landing pad with white lines painted on it. The instructor landed the helicopter and told me I couldn't move on to the next lesson until I mastered the hover. He said the way I was going to do this was by doing "minute drills" around this square until hovering was second nature to me.

I tried for a while, but my grip on the controls was still too tight. Finally, my instructor told me I had to let go a little so that I could feel what the aircraft was doing and make the appropriate corrections. I took my instructor's advice and loosened my grip and, all of a sudden, I was hovering!

I have since learned this is an analogy for so many things in life—letting go just a little can make all the difference.

# CHAPTER SEVENTEEN

# The Legal Battle Begins

After Dr. East's articles came out, I felt angry, and knew a terrible wrong had been committed. I once again found myself stymied. I didn't know how to go about seeking justice.

To be clear, "justice" meant taking Malvonia East out of a position of power so she couldn't do something similar to anyone else. Another option was to change the law—make it illegal to violate the privacy of a research subject.

If Dr. East was licensed to practice psychology, then I could have filed a complaint with the applicable licensing board, but she wasn't.

If Dr. East had been a member of the American Psychological Association (APA), then I could have asked this organization to step in and sanction her. That was a dead end. She had resigned from APA and joined the American Psychological Society (APS), which had no ethics board.

As a researcher, she seemed immune to any redress.

Julian Hubbard and I talked and talked about my options in terms of stopping the unwanted intrusions into my private life. I was uncomfortable with the idea of suing anyone for damages. It seemed paltry to me. Compared to the damage caused to my life, any sum of money seemed like a minor consequence. After considering information from all available resources and after a lot of thinking and emotional strain, I decided the only reasonable option was to file a civil lawsuit. The other option was to let go of the invasion on my privacy, the articles which had been published about me, and Dr. East's forging of relationships with my family members.

I did not feel letting it go was the right thing to do. Some supporters have said I had the mentality of a warrior. Others have defamed me for my choice to take a stand and fight for what I believed was right. I believe I was in a position to fight. I felt I should attempt to save the next person whose privacy might be invaded. And in my case, if I didn't stand up for my own privacy, what's to stop other psychologists from doing this to others? I knew this pattern could repeat itself if I didn't try to stop it.

I made the decision to file the civil suit in my hometown. I knew there were supportive people there.

In a civil lawsuit, money damages are the goal. I intended to make the extent of my emotional pain clear, and to ensure Julian Hubbard would be compensated for his time and effort.

At twenty-five years old, I went to one court hearing in person. As a winged Naval aviator, I was disappointed that my Navy obligations precluded me from regular attendance at the legal proceedings.

I was at a Fleet Replacement Squadron (FRS) learning to fly the SH-60B helicopter. I had some sense that the civil case might be picked up by the media and suddenly become news. I also knew it would be better for me if my commanding officer heard the story from me first.

I stood across the desk from a man about whom I knew nothing. I told him some of the most intimate details of my life, just in case my story went viral. When I was done, my new commanding officer invited me to have a seat. I sat, ashamed and small, and waited for the worst.

"Have you ever heard the word compartmentalization?" the captain asked. I shook my head. He went on to explain compartmentalization was like putting something in a box on a shelf and only taking it out to think about when the time was right. I nodded, understanding.

"If you can compartmentalize this other stuff," he said, "and keep your mind focused on flying while you're here, then we won't have any problems."

I saw the kindness in his face, then in his words. He wasn't going to make me turn in my wings! I stood, smiled, thanked the captain, and waited to be dismissed.

# CHAPTER EIGHTEEN

# Flying Navy Helicopters

I've often said flying Navy helicopters was what I did while I matured into a formidable opponent for Malvonia East. Life at my fleet squadron was often difficult. I remember spending a lot of time complaining. There was one commanding officer who always yelled at people to bring him the "status." Junior officers were known to literally hide under desks to avoid his wrath.

One day while on deployment just off Hawaii, two sailors injured themselves while lowering a hatch, a heavy iron door. The hatch fell on both sailors, and one suffered a broken leg while the other crushed his hand.

I was the junior of the two pilots called upon to medivac these two sailors to the largest ship in the strike group. There, the injured sailors would receive the medical attention they needed. My crew and I had to pick the sailors up from their ship, then make our way to the big ship. One of the two sailors had to be flown to a land-based hospital because his injuries were so severe, and he could not be adequately treated onboard the ship. My crew and I flew to the island of Oahu to deliver the sailor to Tripler Army Medical Center.

As we were making our way to the runway for takeoff, the brakes on our aircraft caught fire. Before we knew it, the ground controllers had dispatched the fire trucks to us. This was a serious and time-consuming situation. By the time my crew and I were headed back to our ship, the sun started to set, and the clouds began rolling in. The group of ships we were assigned to was heading out, and we had to find them and get ourselves back on deck before they left us behind.

My crew and I were exhausted. We had one final mission, which was to land safely on our own ship as quickly as possible.

On our small Navy ship, there was a system that included two steel beams that slammed shut after the probe at the bottom of the aircraft landed in the correct position. Once the beams are closed on the probe, the aircraft is considered "trapped."

My aircraft commander told me I had the landing, and I never wanted to hear the word "trapped" so badly in my life. Somehow, I managed to get it in on the first try, and there was a small celebration in the hangar that evening.

◉ ◉ ◉

After I made aircraft commander, I was assigned to a new officer in charge (OIC) named Narcissa, a female with a reputation for inflexibility. Since I wasn't known for my flexibility either, some people predicted a poor outcome right from the start. Boy were they right.

There was a long weekend for Memorial Day, and I had just read yet another article about Dr. East in which she said Deirdre had had a stroke. It turned out Deirdre had told Dr. East not to tell anyone because Deirdre didn't want me to find out that she was not well. I was all set to go and visit Deirdre. I had gotten back in contact with her after several years of silence. I now knew Deirdre's health was not good and wanted this visit to be a priority. Instead, Narcissa convinced me it was my duty to go to Florida and assist with the Hurricane Katrina relief effort.

The missed opportunity to visit Deirdre was never rescheduled. I will never know whether a visit during a time of illness would have been meaningful to our relationship.

I wanted to help with the Hurricane Katrina relief effort, so off to Pensacola I went. I was assigned a one-day flying mission with Narcissa. We flew a rescue mission as well as delivering supplies. Narcissa was so tough on me that the two aircrewmen came over and asked me if I was alright afterward. We did some good—we rescued twelve people and a cat.

A family of four was in a convenience store parking lot, and there was no one else around. The store was abandoned, and the floodwater had receded just enough to allow the helicopter to make a safe landing. When my crew and I landed, we sent an aircrewman over to ask the family if they needed assistance. He talked to them for a while, using some very animated hand gestures, then ran back over to the helicopter alone.

He hooked himself back up to the internal communication system and informed us that the little girl would not be going anywhere without her cat. Narcissa and I quickly decided to empty a parachute bag for the cat so we could get the family to safety and move on. In the end, the cat took a ride in a helicopter safely wrapped in a parachute bag so he didn't hurt anyone else or himself, and all four family members got to come along.

My crew and I delivered water, searched, hovered, and rescued. Despite the constant badgering I received from Narcissa, the rescues and supply deliveries made it a good day.

◎ ◎ ◎

There was a senior chief boatswains mate who worked really hard for the detachment (the small number of crew members who detached from the helicopter squadron to join the ship's crew for the deployment only) during our time on the ship. As a thank you, a crew I was part of took him flying on the last flight of the deployment. He and I got to talking about the reason I became a pilot. I wanted to fulfill my dad's dream. As we came in for the final approach to drop off this hardworking, battle-hardened senior chief, he keyed the internal communication system and said to me, "Ma'am, I'm sure your dad would be very proud of you."

My tears fell, both for what I had lost and for what I had achieved.

◉ ◉ ◉

Survival, Evasion, Rescue, and Escape (SERE) school is military training designed to prepare servicemembers should they become prisoners of war. A trainee can expect to be hungry, bruised, and humble by the end of it. SERE was a different kind of difficult. University and flight school tested my book knowledge and perhaps my motor skills. SERE tested something else—my character. I drew upon my difficult childhood experiences. I believe I passed.

Failing means an injury or an inability to finish the course. If an action would have resulted in death in a real live prisoner-of-war situation, the staff in charge train the student via waterboard.

If a student resisted for too long, then the staff member might tell the student, "If I break your leg, then you won't be able to escape, and you're basically dead." This was a warning to the student that she was one wrong answer away from the waterboard. Having been threatened with the waterboard once, I learned quickly how to avoid it.

Among the various forms of torture were the boxes. The staff put the students into boxes just big enough for them to be in the fetal position, then hammered a lid in place. While I can imagine this was hell for claustrophobic students, I loved it. No one was yelling at me or hitting me, and I'm pretty sure I just went to sleep.

SERE taught me how to survive on only water for days at a time. It taught me how to navigate using nothing but the features of the land. I learned how far I will go to keep a secret, and how creative I can be under pressure. SERE gave me the confidence no other school or life experience could have offered, and I'm proud to say I stood up to the challenge.

# CHAPTER NINETEEN

# An Awakening

The evening after we returned from the Hurricane Katrina relief effort, I went to the bowling alley to grab something to eat. I ran into the commanding officer of my squadron. We sat down together to have a conversation. He told me that even though I had done everything I was supposed to do, he didn't think being a career Navy pilot was what I was meant to do. He told me, "You can do it, obviously, but I don't think you would really be happy."

He was the first person bold enough to confront me with this truth—a truth I knew to be true but pushed to the back of my mind. I was not meant to be a career Navy officer. As scary as it felt, I knew I needed to separate from the Navy and follow my dream of being a child psychologist.

Soon after, my detachment was sent back to San Diego where we boarded the USS *Ford* (FFG 54). We deployed in place of a ship that was damaged by Hurricane Katrina. We sailed south and took part in counter-narcotics operations for several months. By this time, I had reached my goal of being named maintenance officer of the detachment.

Despite a policy which forbade junior officers from being berthed with their supervisors, Narcissa and I shared a stateroom during the counter-narcotics operations because the ship assigned the living quarters. It was difficult from the start. Not having a place to get away from her made my life more and more miserable.

My maintenance chief called me into the hangar one day with a serious look on his face. He explained that he allowed us to fly several hundred hours past the preplanned maintenance operation. This was serious and could have resulted in serious injury to the crew due to aircraft component failure. It was my duty to make Narcissa aware of the issue right away. The maintenance got done and no one was injured. Then there was the question of who to hold accountable for the mistake.

The CO of our squadron decided I would be held responsible. Normally, the maintenance chief, whose job it was to maintain the logs, or the OIC, who had overall responsibility for the detachment's operations, would have been held responsible. In this case, as the middleman, I was chosen to take the fall for the failure of the system. After we returned to the squadron, I was unceremoniously removed from my position as detachment maintenance officer and replaced. I had to watch my detachment deploy without me. We had all trained together for months, and being left behind hurt me deeply.

I stayed home at the squadron and worked my ass off flying maintenance flights, trying to keep the aircraft up so other pilots could train and deploy for the good of the entire team. There was another lieutenant named Dick who ran the squadron duty officer (SDO) schedule. I could tell Dick hated me. He tortured me by making sure I stood SDO as often as possible while also flying maintenance for the squadron. The day I was taken off the maintenance schedule, Dick announced that anyone flying maintenance flights only had to stand SDO once per month.

Since I was staying home, I decided to start working on a master's degree. I was determined to never turn out like Dr. Malvonia East. I decided to apply for a master's program in theology, the major most resembling morality and ethics in the department. I went to my favorite University of San Diego professor, who told me he would not write me a letter of recommendation for graduate school unless I dropped my case against Dr. East. He knew I dreamed of becoming a psychologist, but in his opinion, I couldn't fight my case and become a good one.

I was crushed. I am hurt by his decision to this day. Overstepping his authority and abusing his power, withholding my recommendation felt like another wrong I had to right.

# CHAPTER TWENTY

# Gary

After returning home from Hurricane Katrina, I met Gary for the first time at a neighbor's house party. Gary and I were living in the same condo complex. I was attracted to Gary right away. He had gorgeous blue eyes and a great smile. I always thought he was attracted to me too. Gary had just broken up with his fiancé, a painful and emotional time in his life. As months went by, Gary and I became friends. While he enjoyed spending time with me, he maintained he did not date neighbors. Gary later helped watch my cats while I was on deployment.

Since he wouldn't date me as a neighbor living in San Diego, I took orders in Hawaii. Once those orders were confirmed, he broke his rule.

I went for a motorcycle ride one day. After I made a stop, the bike wouldn't restart. I called Gary and asked for his help. Later, Gary teased me for needing to be rescued. One thing led to another, and Gary kissed me for the first time.

It wasn't long after that Gary and I went on our first date. I knew exactly what I wanted and didn't care if I was leaving. I was all-in, and everyone who knew me well knew this too.

Gary was less sure. He maintained the *friends with benefits* party line much longer than I did. Gary's words said one thing; his actions said something very different. He supported me, he listened, and he cared. He prioritized spending time with me. Aside from my father, Gary turned out to be the best friend I have ever had.

The night before I left for Hawaii, my efforts to talk to Gary about the very important topic of our relationship went the same way it always did. I poured my heart out, and he claimed we were "just friends."

Gary took me to the airport the day I left for Hawaii. Since he told me the night before that he still didn't want anything more serious, I figured this was the end of things, especially since I was moving an ocean away.

We hugged goodbye at the security checkpoint, and I felt tears falling on my shoulder. I looked up, and Gary was crying. I asked him why, and he said, "If you think I don't have feelings for you, you're crazy."

Video chat was not yet an option back then. Living so far apart, we made plans to watch the same movie and make the same dinner on some Friday nights, in place of our preference—an actual date. There was also a popular messenger program that allowed us to send GIFs to each other, even as we giggled back and forth on the phone. For eighteen months, Gary and I found a way to make long-distance look disgustingly cute.

While I was a Navy lieutenant, Gary was an enlisted sailor. Although we were never in each other's chain of command, we technically should not have been dating according to Navy rules. There were trusted people who knew. Gary and I kept the relationship quiet.

When we visited each other, we didn't go out in public. I couldn't go to command events on Gary's ships or vice versa. Going out to dinner was rare. An opportunity to travel was fun because we got to act like a "real couple."

Looking back, we aren't sure how we got away with it or why we took the chance—but you can't help who you fall in love with. Now, almost fifteen years later—over a decade of marriage under our belts—both Gary and I will tell you—it was worth it. When it's right, you make it work.

# CHAPTER TWENTY-ONE

# Details of the Civil Suit

I have never been in a combat situation. The closest I came was when I flew for the Hurricane Katrina relief effort. There were trees blown over everywhere, resembling toothpicks scattered from their box. There were frustrated citizens firing off gunshots at passing aircraft. Helicopters downed for unknown reasons littered various parts of the terrain as we flew in search of survivors. Many of the homes were ablaze. Desperate people tied down their deceased loved ones—not letting them float away in the water-filled streets of New Orleans—ensuring they'd be found once some semblance of normalcy was restored.

I was filled with a sense of determination as I faced the surrounding danger. I didn't know if I was facing bodily injury, death, or some other major loss. Instinctively, my body responded by preparing to freeze, flee, or fight.

When I filed the civil lawsuit against Dr. East and her co-defendants, I knew I had to prepare for the battle before me. I felt a sense of impending danger, the same somatic response I felt when dealing with the aftermath of Hurricane Katrina.

The causes of action brought against Dr. East and others named in the civil suit included invasion of privacy, defamation, libel per se, slander per se, negligent infliction of emotional distress, and damages. There were several individuals and corporations named as well.

Igor Petty, an adjunct professor at a major Midwest university was Dr. East's co-author of the "Jane Doe" articles which were published in the non-peer-reviewed journal. It was the Institutional Review Board (IRB) at Petty's institution which said no IRB approval was needed because this wasn't human subject research.

Dr. Evillene Thropp, a psychologist and personal friend of Dr. East, also wrote an article published in the same non-peer-reviewed magazine in which Dr. East's "Jane Doe" articles appeared. Dr. Thropp refers to me as "troubled and vulnerable" and an "unhappy young woman." I've never met Dr. Thropp or had a conversation with her. Somehow, she felt she had enough information to make judgments about me.

As far as I know, she based her comments on notes from the interview between Dr. East and Helga. Dr. Thropp, a mental health professional, used a secondhand account of my personality in her article. The trouble with responding to her is that I run the risk of proving her right. Even now, as I consider taking a stand to defend myself, I wonder if I am coming across as oversensitive or perhaps belligerent.

In her article, Dr. Thropp makes declarations about my character. Her article is meant to be a commentary on institutional review boards. She laments how Dr. East and her co-author, Igor Petty, had to withstand the scrutiny of the IRBs at their respective universities. There was some debate as to whether their research constituted "human subject research." It is difficult for me to understand how their research could have been seen as anything other than human subject research. I am human, I am still living and breathing, and I offered up part of my life in the name of scientific research.

A psychologist doesn't get to call herself a journalist whenever it suits her. A psychologist is a psychologist, not a journalist. One may make the mistake of attempting to utilize the First Amendment in an effort to justify Dr. East's actions. It should again be noted that it is somewhat common for researchers to ask individuals to share sensitive parts of their lives in the name of science. The notion of privacy is the only reason one would participate. Removing the promise of confidentiality would deter consent from many potential participants in case reports or other research. If one agrees to allow their information for scientific study, then the confidentiality agreement must be upheld, or we will lose the trust of future participants.

The only time I am free of the laws that bind me while practicing is at the end of the day when I go home. Even then, there are some limitations. I don't get to take a patient's file home with me, publish its contents, or claim I wasn't a psychologist at the time. Moreover, Dr. East was acting in her capacity as a research psychologist. As a professional and a human being, I am always responsible for the potential harm I may cause others. The American Psychological Association (APA) Ethics Codes clearly states: "Psychologists strive to benefit those with whom they work and take care to do no harm." I must always be aware of my actions and how those can impact the other person (or people) in the room. The same should be true for Dr. East.

Dr. Thropp also asserted that my complaint should be disregarded because I allowed Dr. Corwin to use the videos of me in presentations he made around the country. Dr. Corwin was always careful to protect my identity. I fail to understand how allowing *one* researcher access to *one* area of my life grants permission to *all* researchers and *all* areas of my life. I believe I retained my right to anonymity. Second, I am five years old in the original tape and seventeen in the recovered memory tape. The recovered memory tape was not widely shown and was only displayed to a professional audience. Finally, I initially granted Dr. Corwin these rights when I was ten years old. He checked in every few years and reinitiated this assent. I had no reason to ask him to stop.

My accomplishments include being a decorated former Naval

officer and a licensed clinical psychologist. As a psychologist, I believe all psychologists have an obligation to defend the "troubled and vulnerable." I cannot imagine how a psychologist decides which vulnerable souls to treat well and which to label and disregard. I worked hard to get to where I am, and it is disrespectful to define me by my "troubled" past.

The firm which employed the private investigator who found me was also named in the civil suit. This private investigator helped locate Helga. Dr. East used the information he discovered to interview Helga and gain private information regarding my teenage years.

The non-peer-reviewed magazine in which Dr. East's "Jane Doe" articles appeared was also named in the civil suit.

The university where Dr. East worked while she was conducting her research was named in the lawsuit as well.

Of course, I had mixed feelings about filing a civil suit against Dr. East and the others. I feared the repercussions of what I was getting myself into. I understood this was a "David and Goliath" kind of fight, and my odds of winning were slim. I also knew the risks. Lawsuits are expensive—I could come out of this completely bankrupt.

I felt I was being courageous, and the adrenaline rush when I considered the possible victory was thrilling. I felt determined. I knew it would be a long fight. But I had no idea how long.

At the time the lawsuit was filed, I was at my first squadron, studying hard to make aircraft commander. I was preparing for deployment and buying my first townhome. I had met Gary, although we were little more than friends. Many aspects of my life were happy—but I knew this ride would be tumultuous. It would be months before I would see any progress in terms of the lawsuit. I had to put it out of my mind and go on with my life.

# CHAPTER TWENTY-TWO

# The Legal Battle Continued

At the superior court level, I won my case. After discovery and depositions, the first court found my allegations credible. I felt elated. I almost couldn't believe how easy it was. I was naïve to think this may be the end of the whole thing. I would quickly learn how wrong I was.

It should not have been a big surprise when Dr. East and her co-defendants appealed the ruling to the appellate court. Once again, the majority of my causes of action stood. Dr. East's legal team then appealed the case to the California Supreme Court.

Just before the ruling was issued by the California Supreme Court, I settled with Dr. East and agreed to accept $7,500.

Many people have insisted it was a mistake to settle with Dr. East, wondering why I would do such a thing. I was stationed in Hawaii at the time, thousands of miles and an entire ocean away from my support system. I was engaged by then, and the looming possibility of bankruptcy was very real to me. I wanted to protect my future husband and our future together from any negative consequences. The stream of editorials by Dr. East and her supporters seemed never-ending. Julian and I could not match, much less counter, the boundless publicity and nearly unlimited financial resources we were up against. More than anything, I was tired. I had had enough, and I needed the whole ordeal to be over. I mistakenly thought settling with Dr. East would accomplish this goal.

I was not able to settle with the co-defendants, however. The

California Supreme Court ruling was issued. As I understand it, under anti-SLAPP law, only one of my causes of action stood against Dr. East, which meant I was responsible for the attorney's fees for the remaining causes of action. Those attorney's fees totaled approximately $250,000.

Anti-SLAPP law exists in California to dissuade individuals who would file frivolous lawsuits from doing so. It also prevents people from being sued for exercising their First Amendment rights. Based on my limited understanding, to challenge a lawsuit in California, the defendants must show that they are being sued for "any act . . . in furtherance of the person's right of petition or free speech under the United States Constitution or the California Constitution in connection with a public issue," according to California Civil Procedure Code § 425.16 (2019). (See appendix A.) Again, in my view, the defendants claimed their activity was protected under the anti-SLAPP law, involving free speech and public interest.

In my case, not only did one of my causes of action stand at the California Supreme Court level, multiple causes of action stood at both the superior and appellate court levels. This was a major source of my frustration. The California Supreme Court struck down the majority of my causes of action because it asserted that my lawsuit involved protected speech and was a matter of public debate. The cause of action which was allowed to stand stated that Dr. East misrepresented herself as a colleague of Dr. Corwin in order to obtain information from Helga. The Supreme Court ruled that I did satisfy the burden of proof with regard to the anti-SLAPP motion on my claim of intrusion into private matters. The court also ruled Dr. East's conduct, if proven at trial, would be a serious type of misrepresentation. A reporter shading and withholding information when interviewing a news source is one thing—a psychological professional doing this is quite another.

It felt as if the courts were admitting that I was justified in bringing my case forward, but they were still going to punish me financially. It was the death of my financial life for the next seven years, which felt like forever at thirty years old. It also signified the loss of my independence for a long time. While I could not be more grateful to Gary for his support while I was in graduate school, I despised feeling as though I brought nothing to the table financially.

# CHAPTER TWENTY-THREE

# Personal Impact

By the time the California Supreme Court ruling was issued, I had left my first squadron. While I was still a pilot, I was no longer in a flying status. I was only twenty-eight years old. I would never return to the cockpit as a military pilot.

A few months after the ruling, I rushed to the bathroom from my office on base. As soon as the door swung shut behind me, I sank to the floor in tears. There I was, a Navy lieutenant, in full uniform, in the middle of the workday, crying in a heap on the bathroom floor. I had no idea what was going on with me. I had a bachelor's degree in psychology, and I was working on a master's degree in the same. I didn't see that I was depressed.

Two weeks later, I went to medical, where they talked to me about how I was feeling and diagnosed me with an adjustment disorder. Later, on a return visit, I was diagnosed with depression. I tried various medications. The second medication I tried left me feeling like I was losing my mind. I was extremely anxious all the time and for no reason. I participated in group therapy and individual therapy. I tried very hard, wanting those things to be enough. I continued to feel depressed, which interfered with my work.

A quote from my medical record the day of the California Supreme Court ruling:

"Pt is disappointed with the outcome of a long 10-year legal suit given earlier in the morning. She is overwhelmed at work, school, and family visiting at the same time. Her stressors are reuniting with her mother, meeting with boyfriend's family staying at her home, and the conference happening in the same weekend. Pt feels unable to complete tasks at her new job/position and has higher expectations of herself with not wanting to fail or people be disappointed in her abilities. Pt teared in visit making comments that things that were not difficult are becoming difficult for her, unable to process information, and no will to try."

When I spoke to the doctor quoted above, I was dealing with several life stressors simultaneously. Deirdre was in town visiting. Also, Gary's sister and brother-in-law, whom I had never met before, were there. I was helping to plan a major conference at work, and that event was scheduled while all of my guests were in town. The California Supreme Court decision came down right in the middle of all of this. Looking back on it now, I'm not sure how I kept it together. It was a tremendous amount of stress.

For a Navy pilot, an episode of depression can be waived by a medical board. Any subsequent episode is considered disqualifying. At some point during all of this, I was officially disqualified from flying Navy aircraft forever.

My interpersonal relationship skills tanked. I trusted no one. I was angry and depressed, and I was ever-defensive, sometimes playing offense instead. Gary was the only bright spot in my life.

This was the "Viking or victim" mentality—I was so scared of becoming the victim again that I put on a Viking's armor and made sure the whole world could tell where I belonged.

To those who had the misfortune of knowing me during that time in my life, I only wish I could go back and apologize. I was in a great deal of emotional pain. There is never an excuse for treating others badly. I can only say that I was hardly aware of anything going on outside of myself.

I lost all motivation to do my job. Deep down inside, I wanted to care—I just didn't. I was supposed to be making and returning phone calls and accomplishing small tasks toward a larger goal of getting humanitarian relief to a part of the world very much in need—the kind of mission I would give almost anything to be a part of today. I hate myself for the opportunity I missed back then. I was an empty shell showing up to work every day, going through the motions. I was not emotionally present.

I had a migraine which lasted two years. I tried everything to treat it. I took traditional medications, herbal medications, underwent massage and acupuncture. I went to a local college for acupuncture to save some money. I was going every week, and the out-of-pocket cost of nontraditional interventions added up fast. I went for several months and had seen several practitioners. One clinician took full advantage of the opportunity to show his students various techniques at my expense. First, he put twenty needles in my back, then removed them after I had them in my skin for thirty minutes. Next, he showed off his cupping skills. My back looked as though I had two-inch polka dots all over it. Then he lectured me about the bitter herbs I needed to take because "life is a mix of the sweet and the bitter." Even all of this didn't turn me away from nontraditional remedies. Eventually, though, I stopped getting any relief at all from the treatments. I finally just accepted it.

◎ ◎ ◎

My boss at the time hated me. In a meeting once, he admitted it. He had me transferred out of anti-terrorism force protection. Knowing the emotional struggle I was enduring, he assigned me to a much busier and more difficult job.

Ironically, he would later be called to fill in for the head of the entire operations side of the Pacific Fleet, the busiest job in the command. It was around this time that I submitted a request for a hardship transfer, also known as a humanitarian transfer, from Hawaii to San Diego. I submitted this request because I couldn't continue without my support system. The emotional pain was overwhelming.

Had my request received the standard approval, it would have been complete within one or two business days. Two weeks later, I was still checking the status of my request every day with my supervisor. I was very aware that my former boss was the one in the position to approve my transfer request. Finally, I had had enough. I looked my supervisor right in the eye and told him if my request wasn't approved within the next twenty-four hours, then he should expect my grievance complaint to be filed shortly thereafter. My request was approved the same day.

# CHAPTER TWENTY-FOUR

# The Bankruptcy

I returned from Hawaii and settled myself back in San Diego. I had put the California Supreme Court decision on the back burner until a manila envelope appeared on my desk one night at work. I opened it to find that my wages were being garnished (Dr. East's lawyers filed a petition with a judge to take a percentage of my wages to pay their legal fees). No attempt had been made by Dr. East's attorneys, who had also represented the other co-defendants, to arrange payment of the debt. I spoke to the judge advocate general (JAG), a military lawyer. He told me in no uncertain terms that I should file for bankruptcy.

I did an internet search for bankruptcy attorneys in my area. I made an appointment with the first attorney I called. My pay as a single lieutenant disqualified me for protection under federal bankruptcy law. My only option was to get out of the Navy.

I had been in the Navy for a decade, my entire adult life. While I had dreams of being a child psychologist, I was still very much committed to the Navy. My end of obligated active-duty service was a few months away. I felt backed into a corner to make this decision, forced not to renew my service, and it felt unfair. I once again felt as though Dr. East had won. I felt I was wrong for having ever fought Dr. East in the first place. I arranged to separate from the Navy and to file bankruptcy. I told myself that I had to go through bankruptcy to protect the man I was about to marry.

The process of transitioning out of the Navy and into civilian life was difficult in many ways. I was lucky to maintain my base access because I became a Navy spouse right after separating from active duty. I struggled for years with the lack of structure I found outside the military. I never quite figured out who to turn to professionally when life threw problems my way.

In preparation for the upcoming hearing, I stopped paying my bills. It no longer made sense now that I was filing for bankruptcy. I felt ashamed. I had never made a late payment in my life. The phone calls I started getting from creditors were almost more than I could handle emotionally.

Not paying your bills is looked upon negatively by military chain of command, and it often results in poor fitness reports. I walked among my fellow officers, wondering if news of my defaulted payments was public knowledge.

My day in bankruptcy court was pure humiliation. I stood in a line of other bankrupt people, waiting for the judge to review and discharge my case. When my name was finally called, it took less than ten minutes for the judge and my lawyer to review what it took me thirty years to acquire.

The worst part of the bankruptcy was having my car repossessed. I lived in a condominium complex at the time. The repo man hooked up to my car when it was parked in the common driveway, right there where everyone could see. I was humiliated while I cleaned out my belongings. I thought I would be safe once the bankruptcy was filed. The car loan had been a part of the discharged debt. The bank had the right to come and get the vehicle.

People have their cars repossessed every day. I knew the possible outcomes when I started the lawsuit against Dr. East. I believed there was more to the lawsuit than losing a car. I was standing up for what I believed in. When I lost everything, the message I received was clear—the world was a very unfair place. There was no defense against someone as powerful as Malvonia East.

And just like that, it was gone. Most of it, anyway. I found out three years later, after the housing market collapsed, that it was my responsibility to conduct short sales on the two properties I had owned as a single woman. During those three years, the homeowner's association fees on both condos continued to pile up. I was once again drowning, thinking this would never end.

First one, then the other—I watched my properties slip away as they were sold off for pennies on the dollar. I raged against the realtors involved in the short sales. It wasn't their fault. I made the choice to fight this battle, and I paid the cost of losing.

The worst part of all of it was that the intrusion into my life forced me to confront my relationship with Deidre and my possible sexual abuse before I was ready. Processing trauma in my own time—and being in control of my own life—was taken from me.

After my loss to the other defendants, I had no reason or desire to trust anyone. Dr. East had made my worst fears come to life. This character, who had appeared from nowhere, who could not have been anticipated, became the catalyst for loss and despair in my life. Today, when I hear her name or see photos of her, I feel nauseated.

For a long time after this experience, I internalized all the negative emotions I was feeling. My intellectual mind decided the world was not a fair place, nor was it one that wanted to hear my point of view.

During that time, anger was my safe place. When you're angry, people back away slowly. Anger is an effective defense against many things—self-doubt, lack of trust, intimacy issues, and in some cases, ignorance. I successfully used anger as a defense mechanism for years—until I realized the downfalls. I was alienating people who may have been my supporters.

I longed for some relief from the emotional pain I was in.

There would be no white knight in this tale. I had no choice other than to cut my losses and start over.

Gary eventually spoke the words I needed to hear—"how long are you going to let her win?"

I was furious, of course. Gary was supposed to be on my side. Where did he get off telling me when it was time to let go?

The days passed, and I slowly started to see how right Gary was. The longer I stayed angry, the longer I continued to allow Dr. East to have control over my thoughts and feelings.

I realized the game was over, and the good guys had lost. I felt I was sitting alone in the darkness with my pain and grief for months. I waited for someone to do something, say something— anything—that would help quell the loneliness I once again felt. Gary, my only point of attachment to the world, was often deployed and unavailable.

I knew I had to let go of the anger, and for the first time, I wanted to. I didn't know how. The answer, it turned out, was therapy—lots and lots of therapy—over several years and with a few different therapists.

I realized *angry* wasn't who or how I was meant to be. Through many sessions of therapy and long conversations with Gary, I discovered once again that standing up for what is right is simply a part of who I am.

Sometimes the anger still slips back in, and I remind myself that's not what I'm living for. Love is worth living for, not anger, not hate . . . only love.

Now that I am on the other side of my emotional reaction to these events, I remain concerned about what this all means for the psychological and medical communities. I fear the public takeaway will be mistrust in the professionals who use our stories for research. After all, someone with an alternate theory and an ax to grind may decide it would be useful to expose you, uncover some childhood shame, and publicize it. When the professional promises confidentiality, I believe all specialists in the field have a duty to respect that contract. The consequences—if we do not keep these promises—will be severe, and the intellectual loss will be great.

# CHAPTER TWENTY-FIVE

# Moving On

After struggling in flight school, I turned a page once I got to my first squadron. Upon arrival, I was one of five female pilots, although it wasn't a simple gender stereotype that I was fighting. One of the women who came before me had flown an aircraft into the water. Another had come out as a lesbian during the era of "don't ask, don't tell." Another would say she was a conscientious objector before she was to deploy a second time.

I might not have excelled in terms of social interactions. I learned my aircraft, and I learned the missions. I earned the reputation I had as a decent pilot and later as an aircraft commander.

I left the Navy and all the hard work behind to become just another face in the crowd of struggling students. I wasn't prepared.

I was always proud that being a pilot was something I did—it wasn't something I was. This turned out to be a little less true than I realized. I had to let go of my identity as a pilot and accept my new identity as an older student among my cohort.

I decided to apply to a doctorate program in clinical psychology. During my graduate school interview, I had to answer questions about how I would handle being an "older student." This was not something I had considered before, and it felt rather discriminatory to me. My age was not something I had any control over, so why was it okay for the admissions staff to be asking me about it as if it were some sort of liability? I thought, if anything, my life experience should be an asset. It shouldn't be a reason to be excluded from the program.

I felt calm as I answered the questions, confident that I was a qualified candidate. The majority of suitable applicants to this professional school were accepted into the program.

I brought life experience to the table. Once in the program, I would simply put my head down and work like hell to get through it. I wanted to be a psychologist since I was a little girl, and a path had once again been cleared to make my dream a reality. I wasn't going to let anything get in my way this time.

By twenty-nine, I had returned to graduate school, working toward my doctorate in clinical psychology. In my classes, I silently wondered if my professors knew about the civil case—and if they did, who did they side with?

The transition from being an expert in one field to starting over as a student in another was difficult. I hit a few unexpected bumps in the road. For the first year, I was still on active duty, working nights, going to school during the day, and planning a wedding— all while my fiancé was deployed and sometimes unreachable.

There's nothing wrong with being a student. I took a risk to follow my dream of becoming a psychologist—I was proud of that. But the role of student is typically assigned to someone much younger than I was at the time. To transition from feeling very accomplished in one field to feeling like a novice in another is a very humbling experience.

During my time at Third Fleet, I stood the midwatch. The midwatch starts at 10:00 p.m. and ends at 6:00 a.m. Those were long and very tiresome nights for me. I knew it was against the rules when I brought my Rottweiler, Sadee Leigh, to watch with me. Sometimes I would leave her in the car with water and food. Sometimes Sadee came inside with me and sat under my desk. Other days, I would get off work at 6:00 a.m., drive over to the school, crawl into the very back of my SUV, get under the comforter I kept there for just this purpose, and sleep for an hour before my first class. Sadee only went to work with me if I didn't have school the next day.

There were days I wanted nothing more than to give up, go home, and go to sleep. There were nights when I wanted to sneak into the admiral's office and take a nap on his couch.

Somehow, I made it through the first year of my doctoral program. I was able to get out of the Navy and become a normal, full-time, sleep-all-night kind of student whose biggest complaint was too much homework.

# CHAPTER TWENTY-SIX

# That Which Is Not to Be

After the opportunity to visit Deirdre was lost to Hurricane Katrina in 2005, there were two years of near silence between us. Occasionally, there was a telephone call or birthday card, but we did not see each other in person. I was in contact with Deirdre again while Gary and I were dating. Gary and I drove to have lunch with her and Liam once at my insistence. This interaction was difficult. The four of us sat down to eat at a nice restaurant. We ordered, and as we waited for our food, Liam asked me in his slow, drawn-out manner, "So, Nicole, do you remember how old you were the last time you lived with our mother?"

Deirdre instantly piped up, "Liam!"

"I'm just asking a question."

"Well, don't," Deirdre whisper-shouted, trying to communicate how serious she was without making a scene.

We sat in awkward silence until the food came, at which point Deirdre started to help Liam cut up his food.

"I can do it myself," Liam snapped.

"Just let me help you. It will be faster," urged Deirdre.

"Mother, I will do it myself," Liam said with finality.

Deirdre put down the utensils and sighed heavily. The look she gave me was one of embarrassment and frustration.

Throughout the meal, Liam and Deirdre took turns asking me about the past.

"Do you remember the house we lived in on Rumble Road?" asked Deirdre.

"Yes, I think it was green with a big tree in front, and there was honeysuckle growing in the backyard," I said.

"Do you remember when grandma fell down the escalator at the mall?" asked Liam.

"I do remember. It was pretty scary," I replied.

"What about the beach? Do you remember when we all went to the beach?" asked Liam.

"No," I said sadly, not wanting to disappoint either of them.

I was not emotionally prepared for the extent of Liam's cognitive deficits. It struck me then how much Deirdre and Liam wanted seven-year-old Nicole, the little girl they had last spent time with, and not the grown woman sitting before them. I would attempt to engage in adult topics of conversation, while Deirdre and Liam would consistently return to topics more appropriate for a child.

A few months later, Deirdre flew to Hawaii to visit me, and then later met me in San Diego where we were supposed to celebrate my twenty-seventh birthday. This was the only birthday I ever recall spending with Deirdre. While in Hawaii, Deirdre insisted on a couple's massage at the very fancy resort where she was staying. I was less than thrilled, as I felt uncomfortable at the thought of being naked in front of Deirdre. I obliged anyway, thinking this would make her happy.

When she invited me to do extravagant activities like this one, I was used to Deidre paying for them because her resources were much greater than mine. This time, Deirdre paid her half of the bill and left me to pay the rest. I was somewhat taken aback. I said nothing. I paid what was due and moved on with the trip.

Having already scheduled our flights separately, Deirdre and I did not fly together to San Diego, although we both flew there the same day. We stayed at Gary's condo while he was on military deployment. Deirdre promptly made her thoughts on the quality of Gary's condo known to me. She criticized the condition of the couch. Tired from our flight, we sat down, and in a very sarcastic tone, she said, "That's a lovely couch cover." I got the feeling she probably expected me to agree with her. Then she commented on the cleanliness of the condo. I felt very protective of Gary, who had opened his home to us while he was away. I was so insulted, I could hardly speak. This was a bad start to our three-day stay, and things never got better.

Six neighbors and friends gathered at Gary's condo to celebrate my birthday. Deirdre had asked me what my favorite flower was, and I told her it was sunflowers. This became the theme of the party. Deirdre decorated the condo with sunflowers and purchased a sunflower cake. Despite my objections, Deirdre insisted two guests leave the party to buy ice cream. At that moment, I realized Deirdre was throwing a birthday party for a seven-year-old. Having lost custody of me around age six, time stood still for her. Once again, I held my tongue until I could collect my thoughts and explain my feelings.

At breakfast the next morning, I tried to explain to Deirdre, as gently as possible, I was no longer her seven-year-old daughter, and if that's the relationship she needed, I couldn't do it.

"Yesterday was . . . not okay," I began.

"What do you mean?" asked Deirdre.

"You sent my friends to the store to get ice cream when I asked you not to," I said.

"Oh, they didn't mind. It was no big deal." Deirdre tried to lighten the subject.

"You threw a party for a seven-year-old, but I'm not a seven-year-old." I tried to keep my voice steady.

"I just tried to do something nice for your birthday," Deirdre replied.

"I don't think I'll ever be able to give you what you want from me," I said softly.

"And what is that?" she asked.

"Your seven-year-old daughter back," I said.

"Well, if that's how you feel about it, fine," Deirdre snapped.

Deirdre quickly paid the bill and left the restaurant. As soon as I disagreed with her, she disappeared from my life again.

No matter how much transpired between us, I still longed for a relationship with her. My emotions were still open to Deirdre, and I was allowed to be hurt and angered by her actions. I would still say yes to whatever expensive outing she suggested, no matter how silly I thought it was.

Logic simply didn't apply. It was as if I was four years old again, going back and forth between houses for visitation. During that time, when I was with Deirdre or talking to her, I wanted nothing more than to please her. Then, when I was with my father, all I wanted to do was please him.

The difference was that I had what I needed from my relationship with my dad. I would never have what I needed from my relationship with Deirdre. I felt I had my father's approval, his statement of pride, his unconditional love. I never felt I had Diedre's unconditional love.

Deirdre loved me only when things were exactly as planned or anticipated. Deirdre loved me only when I was behaving like a sweet seven-year-old girl and never when I was asking questions or making waves.

Both Deirdre and I longed for something which was not to be. I was born to make waves, and Deirdre was incapable of loving that version of me.

I am not someone who stands on the sidelines when I witness injustices. I have to say something, do something. Perhaps this has to do with my life experiences, or maybe I just learned it from my father.

# CHAPTER TWENTY-SEVEN

# The Proposal

In January of 2009, on Gary's thirty-second birthday, he walked into the living room of the condo we shared and handed me a bag while I sat on the couch. The bag bore the name of a jewelry store, and I was confused. I had been dropping hints for Gary to propose for months. He never seemed ready. On his birthday, I got the proposal I had been waiting for, and Gary got the yes he had been hoping for.

Admittedly, for a long time, I was disappointed by Gary's proposal. This is not a secret to him. This may make me sound shallow. I guess I had been hoping for something more romantic. I also felt as though Gary had withheld a "good" proposal because he was annoyed with me for making it clear that I wasn't going to be his lifelong girlfriend. Perhaps he felt I was badgering him into proposing, and he was frustrated with me. He will deny this if you ask him.

I invited Deirdre to our wedding. I sent the invitations months in advance. The ceremony was a few hours by plane from where she lived.

When Deirdre didn't respond to the invitation, I called her and asked if she was planning to attend. She simply answered, "No, honey, I can't," with no further explanation.

I hung up the phone and looked at Gary. I wasn't even sure why I was so hurt. I hadn't expected anything more, or anything less.

There were so many times Deirdre let me down, and Gary told me to just walk away.

"I hate seeing you get your hopes up," Gary said. "I know it sounds mean, but sometimes I wish you would just give up."

"That's so easy for you to say," I said. "I can't make you understand what it's like to want to have a relationship with the person who gave birth to you because you already have that relationship."

Gary fell silent. He had long since been losing this argument. He knew what he wanted was what was best for me, but he also knew I had to arrive at that place in my own time.

It took years for me to finally understand that I would never have a "normal" mother-daughter relationship with the woman who gave birth to me.

Deirdre came back into my life sporadically, sending cards or making phone calls. But it was never consistent—it took a while before I understood this was the only relationship dynamic we would ever have.

I made holiday calls that went unreturned. She made promises and never kept them. As time continued, more and more feelings got hurt. It never got better. I was reading this map with a broken compass, but the map kept changing on me too. I had to cut the rope and let her go.

◎ ◎ ◎

On our tenth anniversary, Gary told me to pick a diamond ring I liked. He has always been great at picking out jewelry for me in the past. He knew I would want the tenth-anniversary band to fit with the wedding and engagement rings in a certain way, so he left it to me.

We got the ring resized to fit my size-eleven finger. When we got it back, Gary got down on one knee and asked me if I would stay married to him. I finally got the romantic proposal I had always wanted.

# CHAPTER TWENTY-EIGHT

# The Big Day

"We're going to be late," I said, the panic building from somewhere deep within me. If the hairdresser didn't hurry up, I was going to leave without my bridesmaids. In the hair stylist's defense, she really was doing her best to finish the hair and makeup for me and my four attendants. All I could think about was Gary, standing there at the altar, alone. He still teases me about being a half hour late to our wedding.

My maid of honor, Jen, did her best to calm me down. This was ironic because Jen is not known for her ability to self-soothe. I wondered how Jen would handle it if this happened at her wedding, which was coming up in just a few months. The other three bridesmaids were either having their hair or makeup done or fussing in the mirror about dresses and shoes.

Besides the woman doing everyone's hair, trying to avoid my disdainful looks, the only other people in the hotel room were two of my friends from flight school who came to drink and be silly for the day. Katherine and Valerie are both Marines, both mothers, and in my opinion, both amazing. The atmosphere of fun was definitely in place for the day.

There are days in life when I've looked back and evaluated where I came from. My wedding day was certainly one of those days. I had loved and lost for over a decade, and I never thought this day would come. I had learned the true meaning of the word *alone*. Now my life was about to change for the better and for always.

I had found a man who I love with great passion. We were ready to build a life together. I was in awe of the day even as it was happening.

My four bridesmaids and I finally made it to the limo. Gary and I rented a vintage Rolls Royce limousine for our big day. We share a love of classic cars, so this decision was a no-brainer.

Four red dresses and one white piled into a limo, and off we went. A cherished moment, pictures of that limo ride still hang on my wall—Jen and I have never looked happier.

Of course, I didn't see Gary. I could imagine his sigh of relief when the limo pulled up to the ceremony site. We were married at Mount Helix in La Mesa, California. The site included an old concrete amphitheater built into the side of a mountain. At the top of the mountain sits a huge white cross, and on a clear day, you can see all the way to the ocean. Had Gary been late, I would have been livid, unable to mask my fear of his not coming. The limo dropped me off behind the stage, where I was to remain until the big reveal. My veil down, I held only a single red rose.

The rose was a symbol for my dad—I would've moved heaven and earth to have him there with me. My tears fell as I listened to the song playing, a sweet harmony about a woman who lost her father, carrying a red rose on her wedding day to remember him. There was no stopping those tears from falling. This, I knew. I cried for all the moments he missed and for all the moments he would miss. More than anything, I cried for the man I lost and the man Gary never got to meet. I cried the tears of a little girl who missed her daddy.

The song played and I waited, and the memory of the man who should have been there to walk me down the aisle came flooding in.

My dad was born in New York and grew up in the Bronx. He was a jeweler and a Navy veteran. My dad and I had a special kind of relationship, more like two old people bickering than like father and daughter. My dad liked to yell, and I liked to yell back.

My dad would ask me for advice about his relationships, and I would respond honestly. He was not the best at relationships, to be sure. He was married three times, and he dated as much as possible. Even with all the yelling and dating advice, my dad was still larger-than-life to me.

People used to joke that my dad cloned me. We looked so much alike, it was uncanny. I would go with my dad to make deliveries at jewelry stores where he repaired items, and I would just stand there beaming when someone mentioned the resemblance.

I decided long before my wedding day that no one could take my dad's place to walk me down the aisle. I would walk alone—a symbolic red rose my only company.

# CHAPTER TWENTY-NINE

# The Back-and-Forth of Not Knowing

After being interviewed by Eleanor Gordon Smith for her book, *Stop Being Reasonable*, I realized that I woke up every day uncertain about my abuse—and I couldn't keep doing that. Moreover, I didn't want to anymore. That interview was the catalyst, the driving force I needed to change my thinking. I decided to come to terms with not knowing, for better or for worse.

For most of my life, I've been exhausted, my conclusions changing on a day-to-day basis about my mother and the sexual abuse. The most troublesome aspect of uncertainty isn't the change of opinion—it's the implications that go along with it.

I spent most days believing I was molested. On those days, I experienced the feelings of anger, shame, disgust, and grief. I was angry that my body had been violated. I remember sitting alone in my childhood bedroom thinking about this. It was unfathomable to believe that the person who is supposed to care about me the most would commit such a violation. The intensity of the emotion was indescribable. Disgust mixed with anger—it burned so hot, I could barely contain it. Shameful, I would often wonder what this truth would mean about me. I felt broken and damaged, like everyone in the world could see it. These feelings colored decisions I was making in my adult life. I grieved the loss of my innocence and my relationship with Deidre. It was a confusing and lonely place to simultaneously miss both of those things, so interconnected that one had taken the other.

On the days I believed I was hurt by Deirdre, there were still questions. Why would a mother do such a thing? Did she mean to do it, or was she just cleaning me, and she went too far? Did she dissociate? Is it possible she is telling the truth when she says she doesn't remember doing those things?

Any day I considered innocence, I had many other things to consider. On those days, I had to grapple with the enormous emotional burden that had been placed on my biological mother for no good reason at all. I also had to wrestle with what this said about my father. Did he lie to gain custody of me? If so, could I still think of him as a good man? Or worse, was it me who lied? If it was a lie, could I still call myself a good person? There is also my maternal half brother, who missed me tremendously, suffering when I was taken from our mother. Who was to be held responsible for his misery?

How do I live without knowing the answer to such a foundational and fundamental question about myself? I lived in limbo, never really knowing what version of events I would believe that day. The shifting sands of an ever-changing foundation make it incredibly difficult to build a life. I hardly knew who I was or who I was supposed to be. I lacked the metaphorical mirrors to tell me who I was. I felt empty, like a black hole, negative energy constantly swirling inside me. I was lost in a sea of not knowing. The internal struggle, apparently not obvious to those around me, rendered me largely mute, barely able to exist in the mundaneness of everyday tasks.

At some point, I realized I couldn't keep waking up every day wondering what the truth was. For a long time, I decided to simply call myself a survivor of childhood sexual abuse. This gave me an identity, a stable foundation to build my sense of self. I hadn't stopped questioning whether it happened. It was easier to disconnect from the argument and believe I was a survivor.

Dr. East also wrote disparaging things about another woman after a court case in which she testified for the defense. When I decided to come to terms with not knowing, this other survivor of Dr. East panicked. She got very upset with me when I changed my position. Her concern was that I had taken a step toward Dr. East's way of thinking. I made it clear to this person that I was living my truth, not scripting my life to satisfy some narrative. I also don't think my uncertainty gives more weight to Dr. East's position.

People close to me always say if the story wasn't true, it didn't "count" because I was too young to understand the consequences. Of course, it counted. It sent into motion events which left me alone and isolated. It also impacted the way I feel about myself, coloring my relationships for much of my adult life.

I feel as though I did have a sense of right and wrong, even back when I was four years old, and hopefully I didn't lie. I just wish my mind would let me remember.

# CHAPTER THIRTY

# Sadee Leigh

While still in graduate school, I had a chance to speak at the San Diego International Conference on Child and Family Mal-treatment in 2010. This would be the first of a series of talks I would give about the civil case in venues across the country.

To be honest, I was terrified. I was afraid Dr. East would show up at the conference. I would be so scared of seeing her in person that I would hide under a chair. I worried supporters of Dr. East would be in the audience and report back to her. My fear was another lawsuit.

I went to my dissertation chair, an expert in the field of trauma with a voice in recovered memory. I wanted her input on the PowerPoint presentation for the conference. I was anxious to present a clear and complete summary of the events that transpired.

After much preparation, anticipation, and worry, the day finally arrived. Dr. Frank Putnam, a highly respected psychiatrist, presented with Dr. Corwin and me. Dr. Putnam finished his portion of the presentation, and before I knew it, I was standing in front of 200 people, all of whom were staring at me expectantly. I froze.

Thinking back to flight school and other pivotal moments in my life, I looked to the heavens. I began to silently recite the Lord's Prayer.

By the time I finished, I had once again found my resolve. I took a deep breath, looked back at the audience, swiftly said, "Let's do this," and began my presentation. In the end, the audience thanked us with a standing ovation.

I have since stood before audiences all over the country and watched the videos of myself as a young child. I have never gotten used to it. I'm not sure if other people have a similar experience when they watch videos of themselves as a child. I wonder if I am, in particular, removed from my younger self due to the subject matter.

No matter the reason, while the little girl in the video is cute and relatable, I am embarrassed for her, and I have trouble relating to her, unable to wrap my head around the fact that *she* is *me*. Sometimes, I cannot find the string through space and time that connects me to her, simply seeing a smart kid with a fascinating story, a girl who resembles me.

Sadee Leigh sat quietly under Gary's chair while I gave my presentation. At the end of the talk, people were surprised to notice a dog had been in the room the entire time. To be fair, Sadee was a certified therapy dog. As her handler, I could take her to various programs to provide comfort. This time, I needed her.

Typically, at the end of presentations of this sort, people crowd around and ask questions. I didn't want anyone to know how afraid I was. I was afraid a supporter of Dr. East would walk up and start yelling. I felt vulnerable, barely capable of stabilizing the feet beneath me or shaking the hands offered to me.

So, I stationed Sadee right in front of me and gave her the command to "sit." Sadee sat at attention as every person in the room filed past me and either commented politely or said nothing. I was aware Sadee's presence would scare off some people. I didn't want to deal with anyone she hadn't vetted first.

Sadee wasn't so much a dog as she was my canine soulmate. She was the reason I got up in the morning while I lived in Hawaii. If it wasn't for Sadee, I probably wouldn't be alive today, because she pulled me through periods of major depression and thoughts of suicide.

Sadee was also a major reason Gary and I ended up together. When Gary and I were neighbors, I would ask Gary to use his key to let Sadee out when I worked late, letting her run around outside and be free. In all reality, Gary probably fell in love with Sadee before he fell in love with me.

One night, Gary came home after a wedding he went to as a friend's date. I had trouble falling asleep that night, worrying about losing him. Gary used his Sadee key to let himself into my house. He knelt by my bed to let me know he was coming home alone and that my fears were unfounded.

Sadee Leigh Kluemper

All dog owners likely say the same thing about their dogs. Their dog is unique. Sadee Leigh was unique. When I was on the couch, staring off into the abyss, Sadee would go to the front door, look at me, then come back to put her head on my thigh. Sadee would repeat this until I got the hint—it was time for a walk. Sadee somehow knew how to keep me moving through life even when I lost my way.

Sadee was there to cuddle with me during the lonely nights when Gary and I were separated by an ocean. Sadee watched me cry tears of loneliness, tears of heartbreak when the California Supreme Court decision was made, and tears of despair on days when life didn't seem worth it anymore.

Sadee was there when no human being on this planet was.

A few years later, I included a photo of Sadee with the notecards I used while defending my dissertation; the final step of my doctoral studies. I knew seeing Sadee's smiling face would bring me the courage and strength I needed to make it through the most terrifying moments of my dissertation defense. Even when she couldn't be physically present, her spirit was still there with me.

# CHAPTER THIRTY-ONE

# Graduate School

During my time in graduate school, I took a break from my struggles with interpersonal relationships. I was very focused on my studies, which included classes, internships, and my dissertation. I had positive interactions with instructors and my dissertation chair during this five-year period.

My dissertation was titled "Dissociation, Fantasy Proneness, and Suggestibility in Participants with Varying Levels of Trauma Exposure." It was a good fit for me given my history. I compared data in support of the trauma model of dissociation (see appendix B).

I also applied and was accepted to a prestigious APA internship for my final training experience.

I got my PhD four years after marrying Gary. Gary supported me both emotionally and financially through my doctorate program. During my childhood years, school was my safe place. During my graduate studies, both school and home were safe havens, a luxury and foreign feeling.

At the graduation ceremony, I stood next to my friend Anna, with whom I had studied, each in our tam and gown. This was the day we had waited for. Classes, exams, internships, and dissertations were complete, and finally, it was time for the diploma.

I was awarded a final internship in Pasadena, California, finishing the last weeks when it was time for graduation. I came home to San Diego to attend the ceremony. Many graduates had multiple generations of family present to witness their achievements. So many proud parents, grandparents, friends, and other family members were there. Admittedly, I had to remind myself just how lucky I was to have Gary proudly standing there with me. In those moments, I also tried to remind myself how statistically unlikely it was for me to be standing where I was at all.

I was the first in my family to go to college, a huge hurdle to overcome. I had lived through so many micro and macro traumas—my father's divorces, my divorce, the loss of my father, the possible abuse by my mother, the public invasion of my privacy, and the court case associated with that invasion. While so much went wrong, other obstacles could have gotten in my way, derailing me from this exact moment.

I was proud of my accomplishment and everything I overcame to get there. I held my head just a little higher on my special day as I walked across the stage.

For every major milestone in my life, I've created a tribute to my father. Since he couldn't be there, it was my way of including him in the day.

One remembrance I created includes Navy photos of both me and my father and an engraved piece of metal mounted beneath them that says, "Like Father—Like Daughter." When I finished flight school, I framed a custom cut matte to fit every patch I wore throughout my training, and in the middle is a poem to my dad. When I made aircraft commander, I found some craft keys and framed those along with a photo of the aircraft and the definition of pilot in command. When I graduated with my doctorate, I cut a matte to include photos of my dad and Gary, along with the dedication of my dissertation, which honored them.

I treasure these items and still display many of them in my home.

# CHAPTER THIRTY-TWO

# Childless by Circumstance

Jen and I were not exactly fast friends. Jen was ahead of me in flight school, and by the time I got to the squadron, she was established while I was still floundering. I found out later that our squadron-mates predicted Jen and I would either be best friends or hate each other. I smile when I think about how glad I am the former is true. After struggling with relationships, it's a welcome experience to have a positive friendship with a woman.

Jen got engaged before me, although Gary and I had been dating longer. I was jealous. When Gary proposed, I made sure to set a wedding date before Jen's.

Jen and I started trying to get pregnant within a few months of each other. We both struggled with infertility. Jen had multiple miscarriages, and I had one too. I wanted to wait until I finished graduate school, lost the weight, and tapered off all antidepressants before Gary and I started trying to get pregnant. We had done it right, and we were so excited when I got pregnant after only a month of trying. Gary's sister and brother-in-law were in town with their two kids. Gary and I knew I was pregnant for several weeks, although the doctor didn't even want to see me until I was seven weeks along. We decided to keep the news to ourselves until the end of my first trimester.

We were at SeaWorld, and I went to the bathroom and immediately knew there was a problem. Gary's brother-in-law caught the look Gary and I exchanged after I whispered in his ear and could tell what was going on. I refused to go to the ER for several days. I didn't want to face the truth of it. A work supervisor finally instructed me to go to the hospital, so Gary and I went together. I walked into the ER full of despair, knowing the outcome I feared most was coming to pass.

That ER doc tried to convince me everything would be okay. The ultrasound displayed an embryo the right size for how far along I was. Then the ultrasound tech got very quiet. There was no heartbeat.

The doctor still tried to tell me I would be fine and sent me home.

I started having pain at about 4 a.m. the next morning, and Gary and I went back to the ER. The next ultrasound showed the embryo at the bottom of my uterus. I was heartbroken. We had talked about names, followed along on the size chart with how big he or she was supposed to be, and started to adjust our world to include a baby. Gary and I sat in a garden at the hospital and cried together. I couldn't help but think about how unfair it was. I wanted that baby so badly.

We went to see the OB/GYN a day or two later, and the ultrasound confirmed that I was no longer pregnant. The doctor who performed the ultrasound said, "There are plenty more follicles, so keep trying."

Gary and I did keep trying. More than two years passed, and there was not another pregnancy to show for it. I blamed myself because I had gained weight again. Gary and I went through infertility testing to determine whether anything was wrong medically. After the results of the tests came back normal, Gary didn't want me to take the medication the OB/GYN prescribed. For this reason, Gary blamed himself for my not getting pregnant.

Gary eventually decided he no longer wanted children, and he wanted to close the door on trying. With my history of major depression, I had to be careful about birth control and the impact it could have on my mood. Eventually, as he transitioned out of the Navy, Gary decided the most logical option was a vasectomy. I literally had to sign paperwork allowing Gary to do this. We tried one last time to get pregnant the night before, then cried together over the dream we were giving up.

I realized later that I hadn't processed the finality of what Gary decided to do. I got angry, both with myself and with Gary. I didn't expect the emotional reaction I experienced afterward.

I have since come to terms with not being a mother, although sometimes I still wish for a miracle.

The stress of this decision led us to couple's therapy. Every other Saturday morning, Gary and I sit on the couch, waiting for the phone to ring. When his decision first arose, Gary feared I would resent him for the rest of our lives. It took me a while to realize there might be more to this than I thought.

Gary and I had started out both wanting two children. Then two eventually became one, and for Gary, one became none. Gary likes our life the way it is.

Even after Gary had a vasectomy, I still wanted to talk about adoption. Gary tried to stay open to the idea. What he really wanted was biological children—that's what we both always wanted. After many discussions, it just wasn't the right choice for us.

After more than ten years of marriage, we compromised about not having a child. It turns out this is possible, but not in the traditional sense. We considered the opportunities open to us now that we were surely childless.

I've read books about being childless by circumstance, and I've cried the tears of grief over memories not made. Some days, I am *almost* okay with not being a mother. Other days, I get caught up in the unfairness of it all.

# CHAPTER THIRTY-THREE

# Oh, Andi

Andi is a Southern girl with almost as many reasons not to trust the world as me. We met through work in 2015, and the first few years of our relationship were rocky. Our paths crossed when I was obsessed with fitting in, but I had no idea how to do that. I took things very personally. My defensiveness went too far, often mistaken for offensiveness. Internally, I wasn't capable of being a friend to anyone.

Andi and I found ourselves on similar journeys of self-discovery. We shared audiobooks to listen to on the commute to and from work and had meaningful conversations about shame, trust, learning to love, and letting go.

There was something about this relationship that was deeply healing for me. For once, I found myself able to be vulnerable instead of defensive in moments of uncertainty. The vulnerability turned to newfound resolution. The budding resolution eventually turned to courage. The courage found its place in other relationships and situations. I had previously lost the ability to trust people and myself.

There was more to being friends with Andi than just vulnerability. She offered a support system when I needed someone, and I returned the favor. Women—unbeknownst to me—could depend on each other. Helga, Deidre, and Dr. East severed my trust, conditioned me to feel that women were the enemy. My relationship skills were never practiced. Through Andi, my ability to trust, love, and enjoy others was reborn. It took me a long time to prioritize stable, healthy relationships with women. Like most people, I still struggle with insecurities, but my girlfriends are there when I need them.

Having relationships with women has gifted me many victories. I'm able to laugh about the small things. I am secure enough to reach out when I need it. I recognize that distance in relationships isn't always about me. I can be happy for other women and understand their success is not a threat to my own. These are skills I didn't have before.

I treasure my girlfriends now. I know I can reach out to them in times of need and in moments of joy. I am blessed to finally understand the value of having strong women in my life who can help keep this strong-minded woman humble and modest.

# CHAPTER THIRTY-FOUR

# That Which I Will Never Know

My childhood included multiple traumatic events. The custody battle between my parents left me isolated and alone. I lost my father not once but twice—when he got sick and when he died. The alleged sexual abuse was not among those major traumas. When Dr. East came in and focused public attention solely on this single incident in my early childhood, she amplified the original trauma and created a new trauma.

As a result of Dr. East's involvement, I had to recount with extreme accuracy everything that happened to me. I was thrown into a pattern of reviewing the facts, interpreting them positively one day and negatively the next. They called it an intellectual exercise, but it was an emotional one.

I was boundless, unable to build a solid foundation or self-image. I needed definition in my life.

At one point, I reached a personal goal—I saw myself as a survivor, not a victim. I settled into the idea of uncertainty. Whether my memory was correct or invalid, I would never know. I had to choose peace and stability over certainty.

I am a different kind of survivor now. I survived a personal attack by Dr. East. I can take solace in knowing there are others like me out there.

I believe Dr. East is the reason I will never know the truth. All of this came about because Dr. East publicly exposed my case to the world and questioned my memories. That event spurred me to question myself, and media outlets questioned my credibility.

As a result of the back-and-forth, there will never be a relationship between Deirdre and me. While Dr. East might not be solely to blame, it is my belief she should accept some of the responsibility. As I have alleged in court proceedings, she gave me a specific reason to distrust Deirdre by forging a relationship with her while invading my privacy. Dr. East's actions strained an already struggling relationship.

I have not rendered a verdict concerning Deirdre. But Dr. East has muddied the water so much that I'm afraid I will never receive clarity about that period of my life.

I take solace from great philosophers who posited that accepting uncertainty is the highest level of awareness. Blaise Pascal captured this wonderfully in his book, *Pensées*:

> *"The sciences have two extremes which meet. The first is the pure natural ignorance in which all men find themselves at birth. The other extreme is that reached by great intellects, who, having run through all that men can know, find they know nothing, and come back again to that same ignorance from which they set out; but this is a learned ignorance which is conscious of itself."*

If Dr. East's intent was to add to the data of the scientific community, any chance of doing so was lost. The opportunity to use the Jane Doe case to help anyone else who was struggling with these issues was also lost.

# CHAPTER THIRTY-FIVE

# Live and Learn

My first job out of graduate school was a nightmare. I wanted to work exclusively with children, but I didn't think any jobs would be available. Instead, I took the first job I interviewed for, at a community clinic, serving adults with severe and persistent mental illness. It was not a good fit, and I was miserable.

Although my supervisor was nice, she liked to micromanage. As someone who is already very detail oriented, her obsession was overkill. I constantly felt the need to defend myself against her perceived attacks. I had a caseload of well over 100 patients in my three-month tenure there. I was not allowed to stop taking new patients until 65 percent of my patients showed up for their appointments. Patients who needed to see me every week or even every other week were not able to because there were no appointments available.

Keeping up on my notes felt impossible. The stress had started to impact my quality of life. Gary suggested I quit several times. I also had to be available at all times for "warm handoffs" from the primary care providers. This meant if any medical doctor in the clinic thought their patient would benefit from mental health services, I had to stop what I was doing and go talk to the perspective patient.

By the end of my ninety-day probationary period, the tension was very high. As a result, I wanted to leave as much as they wanted me to go. I had an intake with a pregnant woman involved in interpersonal violence (IPV). I was not aware she had a young child at home who witnessed it. My supervisor stated that I should have been aware of this and made a CPS report. I was terminated.

I was both stunned and relieved.

The day after the job ended, I found an advertisement for a job working with children. I interviewed a few days later and accepted the job as soon as they offered it. And this new job paid better than the first one did! I've been working there ever since.

I always had a fear of not being good enough. It is possible this came from a sense of being "damaged" as a child. Trauma survivors often feel damaged and as though they need to prove themselves in some way or in every way. The latter was the case for me. I never felt good enough as a daughter because I didn't take care of my dad after he had a stroke. I never felt good enough as a college student or an officer candidate because I didn't feel like I belonged there. I always felt inferior as an officer and a pilot, even when I received positive feedback regarding my performance. I simply didn't believe I fit in. This message was reinforced later in my Navy career when I became depressed and was transferred between jobs at my shore command. As a graduate student, I felt too old to be part of the crowd. As a therapist, I felt as though I had nothing to offer. I feared I was a terrible therapist for years post-licensure.

This fear was, at times, debilitating. I would walk for every flight and sit down for every session with a gnawing feeling in my belly that this would be it; this would be the time I would be discovered as a fraud.

# CHAPTER THIRTY-SIX

# The Weight

I have struggled with my weight since I was eight years old. Fluctuating between losing and gaining weight was a pattern, and it still is today.

Food became my way to cope with anxiety, sadness, and stress. I tried every diet out there. Some of them even worked in the short term. My difficult emotions held me back. In the end, the weight always returned.

Now that I've processed much of my traumatic past, I strive to be at a healthy weight. While I have more than a few pounds to go, I have come to understand myself. I love myself for my flaws and my strengths.

Like most people, I can be self-conscious about the way I look. But I have made peace with who I am. I no longer chase an unattainable, unhealthy image of thinness seen in most magazines and on most runways. I am so grateful for the real-sized women who have spoken out and made it okay for me to be who I am.

Gary is the chef of the Kluemper household, and he cooks healthy and tasty meals, helping me in my journey to lose weight. I've learned to identify when I am feeling sad, and if I am, I ask Gary for a hug. I know how simple this sounds. Some people can't go to their significant other and ask for a hug, but I can go to Gary with anything. If I'm angry, we talk through it. If I need a distraction, he's there. There is strength in learning to ask for help. I was once too insecure and ashamed to ask for what I needed from others. Now I know better.

# CHAPTER THIRTY-SEVEN

# Coming Full Circle

My work is challenging. I log off at the end of each day tired, and sometimes I wonder if I'm making a difference. Because the need is so great, it feels as though I'm only scratching the surface.

In my current practice, I treat children ages four and up. I generally work with patients with low socioeconomic status, often with a history of multigenerational trauma, and from minority or conflicting multicultural backgrounds.

On my best days, I see the need my effort fulfills. When I see change in the face of a teenager, I'm grateful to have participated. When I see hope in the eyes of a mother of a young child, I am distinctly aware that hope is not only possible but needed.

I've heard stories from my preteen patients who have survived multiple drive-by shootings. I listened to tales of those patients who, on various occasions, have been mistaken for criminals by the police in their own homes simply because of their ethnic background. I have child patients who have watched close friends die in the street. I've seen the empty stare of sexual trauma more than I can recount or comment on here.

Vicarious trauma is real. Sometimes I want to run and hide or scream at the top of my lungs over the atrocities my fellow humans are capable of and for what my youngest fellow humans must endure. There are times when I am glad I did not bring children into this world for fear that they may have had to suffer.

Some may wonder why I continue to do what I do. It's simple really. If I am strong enough to endure it, I should, for the sake of those who might benefit from it. In some ways, it gives my early life experiences meaning. I know I can walk through the fire because I have sat in it and survived it. I know the depths of pain and loneliness because I have encountered it in my life. I am confident that I can help someone else navigate it successfully. This is my gift, and I will use it to help others.

Helping others is the reason I chose to write this book. By telling my story, I hope to inspire people because I believe good can come from bad situations. If just one person reads these words and decides not to give up on her own life, my mission's accomplished.

I hope to change the way the various mental health professional boards handle situations like mine in the future. I want to protect the privacy of scientific research subjects. No one should go through what I went through.

I have longed to tell my side of the story for many years. Others have tried and even come close. No one can tell the story the way I can. By writing this book, I fulfilled a personal goal. I hope to leave a lasting legacy. Taking flight is about overcoming the past.

In recent years, movements such as Black Lives Matter and Me Too have brought to light those abuses of power which have gone unchecked for far too long. I believe what Dr. East did to me was also an abuse of power. This book is my addition to the existing narrative—those in power shouldn't abuse it.

# CHAPTER THIRTY-EIGHT

# Taking Flight

There were certainly times in my life when I felt alone. Truly hopeless. No father. No mother. No family at all. No one to call or reach out to. This is my definition of alone. Alone is more than a feeling. It takes on the qualities of a place. It is hollow and black. It is endless and terrifying. It is silent.

Alone coupled with hopeless is a dangerous combination. I have been in this place as well. I have stood at the edge of this cliff and stared, eyes squinted. I have wailed into the silent night and heard no reply. I have cried tears that were never caught. I have reached for a hand that was not there.

Hopeless is a painful and lonely place to be.

Sometimes a feeling is just a fleeting interpretation of circumstances over which we feel we have no control. There is always a reason to go on. There is always something to be done. There is always hope, even if you can't see it.

◎ ◎ ◎

When I spoke at conferences, audience members used to ask me how I overcame such a complex set of difficult circumstances and accomplished so much. I usually made an awkward joke about being in therapy and moved on to the next question. I really didn't know. In my heart, I know I would not have had the confidence to stand up against Dr. East if I didn't have such a remarkable relationship with my father. My dad gave me the tools to navigate society and stand up to people who treated me unfairly. By teaching me to stand up to him respectfully, my dad taught me to stand up to others. When it really counted, that's exactly what I did. It was my David to Dr. East's Goliath, and I had to fight with all my might.

Fighting Dr. East was so difficult, it left me depressed. If Gary hadn't supported me every step of the way, I would have folded under the weight of my depression. Gary gave me a reason to get up in the morning. He made me laugh and held me while I cried. Without Gary, I would not be the woman I am today.

My faith in God got me through hard nights and even harder days. Although I am far from perfect, I tried to let my faith be the moral compass in my decision-making. I leaned on my faith when changes came and children didn't. I asked God to take the overwhelming and crushing situations, and He always did.

Sadee Leigh, my soul dog, and her successors lent me their strength when my own reserves ran low. Just like Sadee and Sammy, Shelbee and Simon are special dogs with huge hearts and even bigger personalities. I thank God for all of them, as well as Gary and my dad, every night before I fall asleep.

I kept myself distracted with twenty-six years of school, including elementary, middle, high, a year in nuclear power school, three years of undergraduate, two years of flight school, a two-year master's program, and a five-year doctorate program. One part of my brain was traumatized, bruised, pained, and in need of healing. Sitting there watching it heal wasn't going to help me get well, so I did something else instead. I ran to the place I had run a thousand times before when life got too tough—school. One part of my brain sat quietly and let the combination of time and healing do its magic while another part of my brain kept my conscious attention focused on something useful.

I was blessed with my father's stubborn streak. I didn't quit, even when life gave me reason to. Sometimes I made the same phone call every day for weeks. I kept at every task until I got it done. Naturally, from time to time, I really pissed someone off in the process. Overall, tenacity is a positive quality—not entitlement, feeling as if the world owes you—but working hard toward your goals and doing the next right thing.

There is something else, something only I could control. I took myself to therapy and remained open to change. I changed some of my bad habits in my interpersonal relationships. I learned to be a little less sensitive to potential slights. I learned to take a breath and wait a moment before opening my mouth to speak. I learned to let my own brand of humor fill a room.

There is so much advice about how to improve your life. It can be difficult to remember to simply take each day as it comes. That is how I learned to fly—one day at a time.

Despite a strong desire to give up at times, I did not. I would not allow Helga, Dr. East, or anyone else to have the power or control over my life. I can now say with confidence—two decades later—that I overcame what Dr. East did. But on my worst days, I still get caught up in the anger and unfairness of it all.

There are certain truths I cannot know. One of those truths is the exact nature of the incident in the bathtub. I can look at the little girl in the tape, believing something probably happened, but perhaps the action was misinterpreted as a sexual touch. She does not look coached to me. Nonetheless, the girl in the video is five years old. She could be innocently repeating language of a father or stepmother who wanted full custody.

There are other truths I can know. My father was my foundation, and my mother could not be, despite her best efforts. I know that the promises of confidentiality we make as professionals to our patients are larger and more important than any unique case or individual researcher. All of us should hold ourselves accountable to protecting that confidentiality, and Dr. East was wrong to have breached that promise.

Overall, I live my truth, and I believe history will accurately reflect the truth of this story.

I consider myself incredibly lucky. Gary and I have a wonderful marriage. Gary is an amazing, attentive, loving husband, and both Gary and I strive to keep our relationship working for both of us. We have an awesome home overlooking where we got married just outside San Diego, California.

There were many helpers along the road of my life. David Corwin turned out to be a helper at critical moments. Before my hardship transfer from Hawaii to San Diego got approved, there was a brief period when I thought I might be separated from the Navy instead. My first and only call was to Dr. Corwin, who came to be a surrogate father to me in some ways. I know I can always count on his voice of reason to tell me the truth and keep me from losing my mind.

Julian Hubbard has been an unfailing advocate for me at every turn and continues to support my sometimes-ridiculous requests long after any duty to me has expired.

My hometown friend was another person who helped me tremendously. She opened her home to me, made me believe I was capable, and honestly loved me. When she and her family came to San Diego to celebrate my graduation from USD, I made the unfortunate choice to prioritize spending time with another out-of-town guest over her. Looking back, I realize I gave up a family who loved and accepted me for something that felt good in the moment. I can never undo the pain I caused her. I am truly sorry for the way I treated her.

When I was at Nuclear Power Training Command, a chief I'll call MMC Davidson helped me. I believe he saw something in me, and he kept me from getting in my own way several times. For example, I thought it would be a good idea to get my ears pierced a third time just below the cartilage before I left active duty to go to USD. MMC Davidson was on duty and saw me walking to study in the school building one evening. Even though we were allowed to study in civilian clothes, basic military grooming standards still had to be followed. He looked at my ears and held up one arm; then, he pointed me back to my barracks to take the earrings out. No words even had to be exchanged.

There was a professor at USD, aside from the one who later refused to write me a letter of recommendation, who was my ally; I'll call him Dr. Cobb. This teacher listened and supported me long past his published office hours. He was the encouragement I needed when times were dark.

The executive officer (XO) of the Air Force training command was a huge source of inspiration during my time there and years later. He never gave up on me. Years later, I was out flying with a senior pilot, and we had to make a stop at the aircraft carrier. The XO from the Air Force training command was now the air boss of the aircraft carrier we were headed to. The senior pilot let me make the check-in radio call, and the Air Boss himself got on the radio and confirmed I was the co-pilot of the aircraft. "Say co-pilot's last name." I did, and we got quite the welcome. I believe it was one of the few times I impressed the senior pilot I was flying with.

The XO of Helicopter Training Squadron 18, Commander (CDR) Williams, was another supporter of mine when the chips were down. He always had positive words for me, even when I made a mistake. I was promoted to Lieutenant, junior grade (O-2), on the same day I received my wings as a naval aviator. I was proud to have CDR Williams read me my oath of office.

CDR Lewis was the commanding officer of my fleet squadron for a significant portion of my time there. CDR Lewis entrusted me with responsibilities that furthered my belief in myself. When things went very badly with Narcissa, CDR Lewis was the one who ultimately decided to fire me as maintenance officer of the detachment. CDR Lewis allowed me space to recover and then continued to rely on me instead of giving up on me. This continued interaction kept me afloat despite my heartbreak over losing my position as maintenance officer of the detachment.

CDR Morris at Third Fleet allowed me to stand the midwatch so I could start my doctorate program during the day and transition back to civilian life.

Dr. Dalenberg was my dissertation chair and mentor during my doctorate program at Alliant International University, San Diego. If it hadn't been for Dr. Dalenberg, I'm not sure what would have become of me. She always had my back, even after I graduated and was licensed. To this day, Dr. D is someone I can go to for a sanity check on major life decisions.

More recently, I've found value in having an attitude of gratitude. I heard this adage so many times over the years and was not yet ready to embrace its power. When I turn my consciousness toward what I am grateful for, my attitude is better, my mood is more positive, my interactions with others are easier, my work is less difficult . . . and life is just *better.*

I have great friends who support me, laugh with me, and challenge me to be my best self. While no job is perfect, I have it pretty good. I work as a child psychologist in a small community clinic in San Diego with underserved patients. I am able to do everything I ever wanted to do as a psychologist—therapy, assessment, and supervision. There is little I want in terms of my career.

I look toward my future and the opportunity to apply the knowledge I've gained through a lifetime of perseverance. I spent a lot of time earning my wings, and now it's time to *See Jane Fly!*

Under the statute, the rights of free speech or petition in connection with a public issue appear to include four categories
of activities: statements made before a legislative, executive or
judicial proceeding; statements made in connection with an issue
under consideration by a governmental body; statements made in
a place open to the public or a public forum in connection with an
issue of public interest; and any other conduct in furtherance of
the exercise of free speech or petition rights in connection with "a
public issue or an issue of public interest." § 425.16(e).

A causal link between trauma and dissociation has long been as-sumed. This model is often referred to as the Trauma Model of Dissociation. According to this model, dissociation increases im-mediately after known trauma, then decreases over time. Evolu-tionary perspective: dissociation serves to protect from potential-ly traumatic event, thus increasing likelihood of survival after the event. In the last decade, some researchers have begun to ques-tion the more traditional causal link between trauma and disso-ciation. These authors believe some people are inherently fantasy prone. They also believe fantasy proneness leads to dissociation and suggestibility, which in turn leads to trauma reporting. This is often referred to as the Fantasy Model of Dissociation. There is some empirical support for this model. Both dissociation and fan-tasy proneness appear to correlate with suggestibility, although the effect sizes appear to be quite variable.

In my dissertation research, I setup a direct test of the rela-tionship of suggestibility to the fantasy proneness and dissociation interaction. This tests the hypothesis that dissociation itself is a risk factor for false or suggestible reporting, which is the Fanta-sy Model prediction. The findings were in support of the Trauma Model of Dissociation, as trauma did relate to dissociation, even when fantasy proneness was controlled. Also, fantasy proneness did relate to dissociation. Finally, dissociation does not appear to be positively related to suggestibility.

## ACKNOWLEDGMENTS

Jo Ann, I thank you for being an awesome writing coach. Thank you for putting up with my stubbornness even when you were right.

Julian, I cannot thank you enough for your time and dedication to my continued well-being. You are an amazing man.

Dr. Dalenberg, Dr. Olafson, Vicki, Dave, Ruth, Dr. Ford, Dr. Boat, Dr. Sonne, Kristen, and Andi—thanks for taking the time to read my manuscript and provide useful feedback during what was a very challenging time for me.

## REFERENCES

American Psychological Association (2017). "Ethical Principles of Psychologists and Code of Conduct."

Pascal, Blaise. "Pensées." New York: E.P. Dutton, (1958), 1623-1662.